As one of th ablished
 brands,
 travel.

 our
 ets
 d,
 aith of
 sion for travel.

 ely on Thomas Cook as your
 velling companion on your next trip
and benefit from our unique heritage.

Thomas Cook **pocket** guides

NOTTINGHAM

Your travelling companion since 1873

Written by Rebecca Ford

Published by Thomas Cook Publishing
A division of Thomas Cook Tour Operations Limited
Company registration no. 3772199 England
The Thomas Cook Business Park, Unit 9, Coningsby Road,
Peterborough PE3 8SB, United Kingdom
Email: books@thomascook.com, Tel: +44 (0) 1733 416477
www.thomascookpublishing.com

Produced by Cambridge Publishing Management Limited
Burr Elm Court, Main Street, Caldecote CB23 7NU
www.cambridgepm.co.uk

ISBN: 978-1-84848-469-6

This first edition © 2011 Thomas Cook Publishing
Text © Thomas Cook Publishing
Cartography supplied by Redmoor Design, Tavistock, Devon
Map data © OpenStreetMap contributors CC-BY-SA, www.openstreetmap.org,
www.creativecommons.org
Transport map © Nottingham Tram Consortium

Series Editor: Karen Beaulah
Production/DTP: Steven Collins

Printed and bound in Spain by GraphyCems

Cover photography © Thomas Cook Publishing

CONTENTS

SYMBOLS KEY

The following symbols are used throughout this book:

ⓐ address ☏ telephone ⓦ website address ⓔ email
⏲ opening times ⓝ public transport connections ❶ important

The following symbols are used on the maps:

𝒊	information office	▨	point of interest
✈	airport	O	city
✚	hospital	O	large town
🛡	police station	○	small town
🚍	bus station	═	motorway
🚆	railway station	—	main road
Ⓣ	tram	—	minor road
✝	cathedral	—	railway
❶	numbers denote featured cafés, restaurants & venues		

PRICE CATEGORIES

The ratings below indicate average price rates for a double room per night, including breakfast:
£ up to £75 ££ £75–100 £££ over £100
The typical cost for a three-course meal without drinks, is as follows:
£ up to £15 ££ £15–25 £££ over £25

▶ *There's more to the city than its famous heroic outlaw ... honest!*

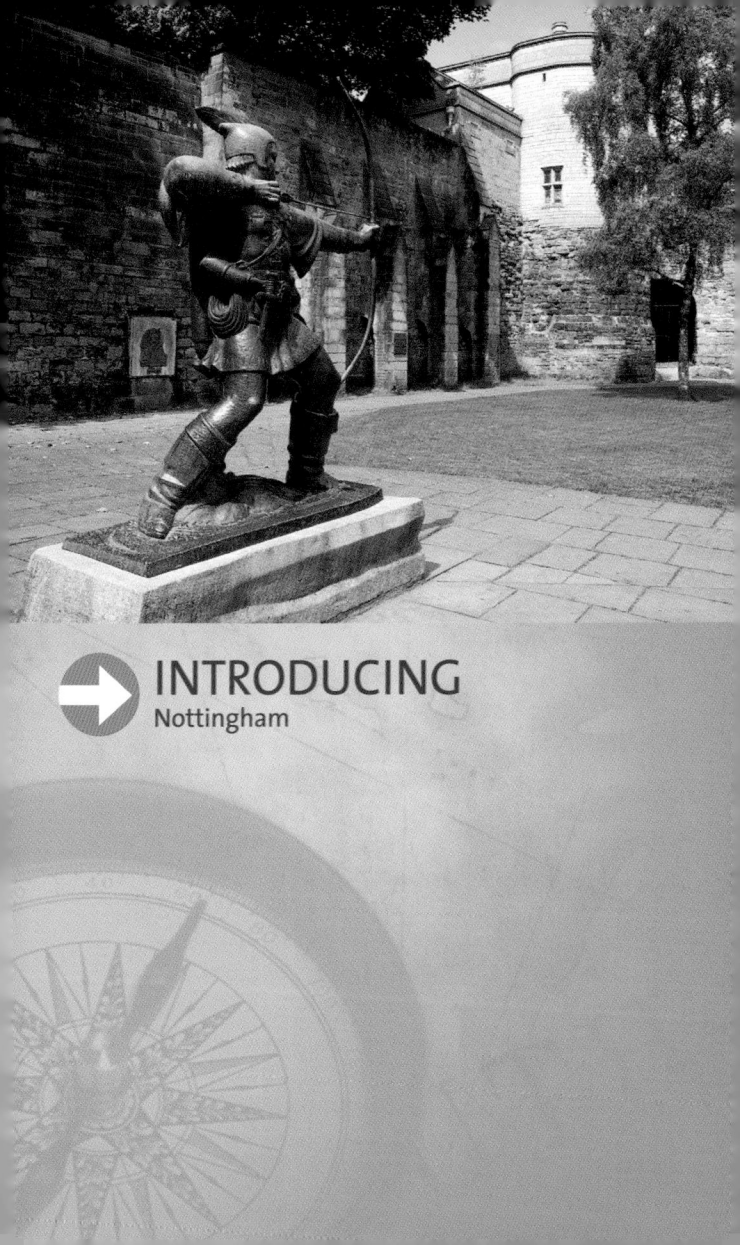

INTRODUCING
Nottingham

Introduction

If you thought that there was little more to Nottingham than its castle, Robin Hood and Brian Clough, then think again. This city, perched upon a honeycomb of caves beside the River Trent, combines rich history with youthful vigour. It has pretty much everything you could possibly want for a great weekend break. There are museums and galleries, some eye-catching architecture, historic churches, friendly people, a good choice of shops and a clutch of excellent restaurants. It's a place where you can admire rare alabaster carvings and paintings by L S Lowry, then stroll across town and buy the latest designer clothes, before sipping a cocktail or two in a fashionable bar. If sport is more your thing, you've got the choice of watching top-class football or cricket, going ice-skating or even getting a rush of adrenalin white-water rafting.

One of the best things about Nottingham is its energy. Here is a city that isn't afraid to embrace the new – or to buck convention. This is a legacy, no doubt, of its industrial heritage (it was once a world leader in lace-making), allied to the entrepreneurial spirit that made it the birthplace of Boots the chemist, Players cigarettes and Raleigh bicycles, and the homeland of fashion designer Paul Smith. Today its vigour comes from the presence of two universities, of which the University of Nottingham attracts students from across the world and has campuses in both China and Malaysia.

In recent years the city centre has received a facelift with the redevelopment of the Old Market Square, which now has a water feature designed by the architects who created the Diana

Memorial Fountain in London, and the addition of the striking new art gallery, Nottingham Contemporary, which has brought a blast of creative edginess to the local landscape. However, the most surprising aspect of the city to the visitor is surely the presence of the Victorian brick buildings, designed by eccentric local architect Watson Fothergill, which combine elements of the gothic and the medieval with a 19th-century confidence that really catches the eye.

🔺 From lace to modern-day design: the city has long been a hub for fashion

When to go

SEASONS & CLIMATE

Nottingham has something to offer all year round. The climate, like the rest of the Midlands, is generally rather cooler than that of London but it is warmer than the more northerly counties such as Yorkshire and Northumbria. As with anywhere else in Britain you should be prepared for rain at any time of year.

The city gets much quieter during university vacations, so you might find it less crowded in the height of summer than you'd expect. During the summer months you can enjoy dining outside, when many of the city's bars and restaurants seem to turn into European-style pavement cafés. In winter, you can wrap up warm and enjoy the city's Christmas celebrations – which have in the past included a giant outdoor ice rink in the Old Market Square.

ANNUAL EVENTS

A vibrant and outgoing city, Nottingham plays host to special events pretty much all year round. The darkness of February nights is enlivened by **Nottingham Light Night** (ⓦ www.lightnight.co.uk/nottingham), an annual light show focused on the castle but with installations and performances across the city. Then in springtime the **City Pulse** festival brings music to the city centre on May Bank Holiday. Summer and early autumn see a colourful range of festivities, with **open-air theatre** at the castle running from June until the end of August and, in July, **Mela** (ⓦ www.asianarts.org.uk), an Asian arts festival, and **Nottingham Pride** (ⓦ www.nottinghampride.co.uk), the city's lively LGBT festival. In August enjoy **Riverside** on the Victoria Embankment – a festival of music and theatre with fireworks and a street fair – and, for all the family, the week-long swashbuckling **Robin Hood Festival** (think entertainers, minstrels, archery tournaments and jousting contests). September celebrates Nottingham's most famous writer, at the **D H Lawrence Festival** in Eastwood, while the city centre becomes a focus for a tasty tribute to local produce in the annual **Food and Drink Festival**. It's all the fun of fair in October when the **Goose Fair** comes to town – one of the city's most ancient traditions.

🔺 *Old Market Square plays host to a variety of events throughout the year*

History

Prior to the Norman Conquest, the Anglo-Saxon town was known as 'Snotingeham' – the homestead of the Snots. Thankfully, when the Normans invaded, built the first castle and established their own settlement here, they dropped the letter 's'. Initially the Saxon and Norman towns were separate entities, divided by a wall but with a shared central marketplace. It was not until around the 13th century that a common town wall was built and the French and English boroughs united.

Nottingham's castle was a formidable hilltop fortress. This, together with the town's location at the very heart of England,

🔺 *Nottingham Castle's commanding gatehouse*

meant that it played a significant role in national life. In 1642 Charles I raised his standard on a hill beside the castle, heralding the start of the bloody Civil War.

Fifteenth-century Nottingham was a centre for alabaster carving, and the surrounding countryside was found to be rich in coal. But it was lace that really made the town's name. In 1808 John Heathcoat invented the first lace-making machine – and a few years later John Leavers came up with a version that could create delicate patterns in the weave. By the mid-1800s there were over 130 lace factories in Nottingham.

Lace fell out of fashion after World War I, but Nottingham had other industries that kept it prosperous: Boots the chemist, Raleigh bikes and Players cigarettes. The late 20th century brought new challenges – local coalfields closed for one thing – but the city is once again a place for innovation and creativity with two thriving universities (development of the MRI scanner was carried out here), a stunning contemporary art gallery and a lively population.

A PLACE OF CAVES

It was around AD 900 when a Welsh monk visited the area that is now Nottingham and discovered a landscape riddled with caves. These weren't naturally occurring but had been carved into the soft sandstone rock by humans. No one knows whether people lived in the caves at that time, but they did become homes in later years. Troglodyte living wasn't banned in Nottingham until the 19th century.

Culture

There's far more to Nottingham than the legend of Robin Hood, and the city has a rich cultural scene – especially since the opening in 2009 of the art gallery, Nottingham Contemporary (see page 49). With two theatres – the Theatre Royal and the Playhouse – and a concert hall, you'll be able to see the latest West End plays as well as classical dramas, concerts and recitals. Among the city's attractions, the award-winning Galleries of Justice Museum (see page 48), with its illuminating exhibits on crime and punishment through the ages, stands out.

Sadly, although the city has a rich industrial heritage, there are few reminders of the mighty 19th-century lace industry in its museums. Working-class times are, however, brought vividly to life in the works of the city's most famous novelists – D H Lawrence, who came from the nearby mining town of Eastwood, and Alan Sillitoe.

Musically, Nottingham's Trent FM Arena (see page 55) attracts big-name international stars, while its sporting pedigree is top class – well, this is the home of Trent Bridge Cricket Ground, and legendary football manager Brian Clough was one of the city's most famous sons.

● *Cafés line the streets of Nottingham's city centre*

MAKING THE MOST OF
Nottingham

Shopping

Whether you're a fashionista on the hunt for the hottest designer dress, or an indie music fan with a love of classic vinyl discs, you'll be able to find shops to please you in Nottingham. This compact city houses all the big high-street names alongside plenty of individual shops. There are three central shopping malls. The **Victoria Centre** is the largest and has a branch of John Lewis, while **Westfield Broadmarsh** is home to BHS. The **Exchange Arcade** in Nottingham Council House is the smallest but the most chic, with quality clothes shops gathered beneath a lavishly decorated neo-classical dome.

Clothes and shoe shoppers should head for Bridlesmith Gate, a pedestrianised street that's lined with upmarket chains like Hobbs, Kurt Geiger, Jigsaw and Ted Baker. On nearby Low Pavement is designer Paul Smith's flagship store, while Vivienne Westwood has a shop in the **FH Mall** close to the Old Market Square. Vintage clothes lovers aren't forgotten either, with outlets dotted around the city. Quirkier, individual shops are to be found along the Mansfield Road (especially good for its jumble of second-hand record stores), and the Derby Road (which has homeware and antiques).

If you're looking for a gift, how about Nottingham lace, which is still manufactured at a couple of places in the county. The **Nottingham Tourism Centre** (ⓐ 1–4 Smithy Row) sells tablecloths, decorative panels and even lace garters.

There's a Farmers' Market held on the third Friday and Saturday of each month in the Old Market Square. Here you'll find anything from ostrich burgers to fresh vegetables.

Shops are generally open 09.00–17.30 Mon–Sat, with late opening on Wednesdays until around 19.00 or 20.00. Most large stores also open on Sundays 10.00–16.00. Some smaller shops close on Mondays.

⬥ *The Exchange Arcade's elegant interior*

Eating & drinking

Although there are no distinctive regional dishes associated with Nottingham, the south of Nottinghamshire is noted for its production of Stilton, considered by many to be the finest of all English cheeses. The Vale of Belvoir dairies in Colston Bassett and Cropwell Bishop still follow an original 18th-century recipe. Look out for it on restaurant cheeseboards.

Given the profusion of Italian-style chains in the city centre, you might be forgiven for thinking that pizza and pasta made up Nottingham's traditional cuisine. However, there are also plenty of pubs serving classic English favourites such as fish and chips, sausage and mash, steak pie and the traditional Sunday lunch of roast beef with Yorkshire pudding. The city has Indian, Thai, Chinese, Japanese, French and Mexican restaurants too, so you won't be short of choice.

◐ *Alfresco dining in the heart of the city*

For bars and popular high-street eateries, make for Chapel Bar or Forman Street. Broad Street and Goose Gate are particularly good for wine bars and relaxed bistros and cafés, while Castle Gate and High Pavement both have some top-quality restaurants. Those who want to dine at the best of these but are on a limited budget should check out their lunchtime set menus, which usually offer two or three courses at a low price. If it's a fine day and you fancy a picnic, make for the grounds of the castle (see page 70) or the Arboretum (see page 56). Alternatively you can munch your sandwiches beside the water feature in the Old Market Square, or sit under a tree in the little garden beside St Peter's Church.

MINE'S A PINT

Beer lovers will be sure to want to check out Nottingham's locally brewed beers. The **Nottingham Brewery** (☎ 0115 942 2649 ⓦ www.nottinghambrewery.com) is a micro-brewery situated at the Plough Inn, Radford, producing traditional cask ales such as Sooty Oatmeal Stout, and some seasonal special brews. The city's largest brewery is **Castle Rock** (ⓦ www.castlerockbrewery.co.uk), which was founded by a former chairman of CAMRA (Campaign for Real Ale). Look out for its ales such as Screech Owl, Harvest Pale and Hemlock Bitter. It also runs brewery tours at its new site on Queens Bridge Road. You'll be able to watch beer being brewed, pour a pint and taste the produce (☎ 0115 985 1615 for more information).

Entertainment

With two universities and a large youthful population, it's not surprising that Nottingham really knows how to party. The city is full of bars, pubs and restaurants that start filling up from the early evening and become progressively more crowded throughout the night. Lively hubs are the Chapel Bar area, near the Old Market Square, and Broad Street and Goose Gate in Hockley. From around 23.00 people start moving on to clubs, of which the city has several, including cool The House of Coco Tang on Bridlesmith Gate (see page 77).

There's something to do every night of the week – and it's certainly not all student oriented. The Nottingham Playhouse (see page 78), the Theatre Royal and Royal Concert Hall (see page 66 for both) all have lively programmes that include plays, musicals, opera, ballet, concerts and comedy. Purchase tickets from individual box offices. In the summer, the grounds of Nottingham Castle are turned into an open-air theatre, where you can bring a chair and a picnic and enjoy an alfresco production.

In winter, the Old Market Square (see page 56) is usually transformed into an ice rink and lively Christmas market, while a giant Ferris wheel arrives for a few weeks around Easter. In the school summer holidays, 300 tons of sand transform the square into a beach – complete with paddling pools and a pier.

The Trent FM Arena (see page 55) hosts big music acts like Simply Red, the Scissor Sisters and Michael Bublé, as well as providing a stage for large-scale events – think *Strictly Come Dancing on Tour* and Cirque du Soleil.

⬥ *A popular venue for big-name bands*

Sport & relaxation

The legendary football manager Brian Clough helped to make sport synonymous with Nottingham – a city that also boasts associations with Olympic ice-dancing stars Torvill and Dean and the Olympic swimmer Rebecca Adlington.

The River Trent divides the grounds of Nottingham's football teams. On the north bank is the Meadows Lane ground of **Notts County FC** (tickets ☎ 0115 955 7204 ⓦ www.nottscountyfc.co.uk), the world's oldest league club, founded in 1862. On the south bank, facing Notts County, is the City ground of **Nottingham Forest FC** (tickets ☎ 0871 226 1980 ⓦ www.nottinghamforest.co.uk). Founded in 1866, the club was managed for many years by Brian Clough.

Also on the south bank of the Trent is **Trent Bridge Cricket Ground** (☎ tickets 0844 811 8711 ⓦ www.nottsccc.co.uk), the home of Nottinghamshire County Cricket Club and one of the world's most famous cricket grounds. Dating back to 1838, it has

RIVERSIDE WALK

The Big Track is the name given to a 16-km (10-mile) walkway/cycleway that runs between Trent Bridge and Beeston Lock, taking you beside the River Trent and Nottingham's 18th-century canal. It's a great way to see some of the city's remaining industrial heritage, as well as its wildlife. For more information and a map contact The Big Wheel ☎ 0115 950 7845 ⓦ www.thebigwheel.org.uk

a library with the world's largest collection of cricketing books. Tours take place every Tuesday at 14.00, lasting 90 minutes. To book call ☎ 0115 982 3000.

In the Lace Market area, the **National Ice Centre** (☎ 0115 853 3000 🌐 www.national-ice-centre.com), opened by Jayne Torvill in 2002, boasts twin Olympic-sized ice rinks. The centre has public skating sessions and lessons, and is the place to come to watch ice hockey games – as well as occasional shows.

Outside the town centre at Holme Pierrepont, is the **National Water Sports Centre** (☎ 0115 982 1212 🌐 www.nwscnotts.com), where you can enjoy splashy adrenalin-fuelled activities such as white-water rafting and water skiing, as well as canoeing, kayaking and sailing. There are both taster sessions and courses available.

🔺 *Nottingham Forest FC inspires a loyal fan base*

Accommodation

Accommodation in Nottingham is dominated by mid-range chain hotels, which offer reasonably priced but generally bland rooms. However, the city does have a number of more characterful places to stay that are well worth trying – although they do tend to get booked up quickly. Accommodation is dotted around the city centre, though many bigger names are concentrated around Maid Marian Way, with others on Derby Road and Mansfield Road.

There are also a number of good B&Bs that are slightly less central, but offer very good value. If you prefer to be more independent, or are staying in the city for a few days, then serviced apartments are well worth considering. There are several in the city, offering many of the benefits of a hotel with the flexibility of self-catering.

Outside the city centre, in the Nottinghamshire countryside, there is a choice of accommodation ranging from country house hotels to farm B&Bs. For longer stays and to add another dimension to your holiday, you could even opt to hire a canal boat (see page 88).

HOTELS

Holiday Inn Nottingham £ With plenty of parking, free Wi-Fi and conference facilities, this canal-side hotel offers modern accommodation just a 15-minute walk from the city centre. ⓐ Castle Bridge Road, Castle Marina Park ⓣ 0115 993 5000 ⓦ www.nottingham.holiday-inn.com

Ibis Nottingham Centre £ This budget hotel is conveniently located on the edge of the Lace Market area, and close to Nottingham Contemporary and shops. ⓐ 16 Fletcher Gate ⓣ 0115 985 3600 ⓦ www.ibishotel.com

Waltons Hotel ££ A former hunting lodge, situated just within the exclusive Park area of Nottingham, this hotel has 17 individually decorated rooms and plenty of original features. There's a restaurant, and a large terrace where you can relax with drinks. It's about a five-minute bus ride from the city centre. ⓐ 2 North Road, The Park ⓣ 0115 947 5215 ⓦ www.waltonshotel.co.uk ⓝ Bus: 34, 35

Hilton Hotel ££–£££ Built as a hotel in 1901 beside what was previously Victoria station (now a shopping centre), this Hilton is very handy for the Theatre Royal, as well as for the lively bars and restaurants of Broad Street. It's a good choice if you like to keep fit, as the hotel boasts a well-equipped health club and a swimming pool. ⓐ Milton Street ⓣ 0115 934 9700 ⓦ www.hilton.co.uk ⓝ Bus: 35, 37

Lace Market Hotel ££–£££ A former Georgian townhouse and later a lace mill, the Lace Market is now a boutique hotel. The bedrooms are decorated in contemporary, fuss-free style and muted colours. The hotel also has an award-winning restaurant and a cocktail bar. It's very close to Nottingham Contemporary. ⓐ 29–31 High Pavement, Lace Market ⓣ 0115 852 3232 ⓦ www.thefinessecollection.com ⓝ Tram: Lace Market

Park Plaza ££–£££ This central four star hotel has light and spacious modern rooms equipped with flatscreen satellite televisions and Wi-Fi. There's a fitness centre on the 11th floor and a restaurant too, although the hotel is just a couple of minutes' walk from all the bars and bistros of Chapel Bar.
ⓐ 41 Maid Marian Way ⓣ 0115 947 7200
ⓦ www.parkplazanottingham.com ⓝ Tram: Old Market Square

Harts £££ A thoroughly contemporary hotel, built to an award-winning design in 2002 in the exclusive Park area of the city. It's just a short walk from Nottingham Castle. Bedrooms offer understated luxury, with some opening onto the hotel's private gardens. Harts has an acclaimed restaurant that serves innovative food. ⓐ Standard Hill, Park Row ⓣ 0115 988 1900
ⓦ www.hartsnottingham.co.uk ⓝ Bus: 13, 14; Tram: Old Market Square

B&BS

Greenwood Lodge City Guest House ££ With a small garden and country-house style rooms, this acclaimed guest house in a Victorian property just outside the city centre, makes a tranquil base. Breakfast is taken in the conservatory. ⓐ 5 Third Avenue, Sherwood Rise (off Mansfield Road) ⓣ 0115 962 1206
ⓦ www.greenwoodlodgecityguesthouse.co.uk ⓝ Bus: 88, 89

SERVICED APARTMENTS

Premier Apartments £ Situated in a modern block close to the Ice Centre and Arena, these one- and two-bedroom apartments all have well-equipped kitchens and sitting rooms with TVs.

One-night stays are available and linens and toiletries are provided. ⓐ The Ice House, Belward Street ⓣ 0115 908 2000 ⓦ www.premierapartmentsnottingham.com ⓥ Bus: 21, 23, 45

SACO Apartments ££–£££ Worth considering if you're staying any length of time in the city (the price per night drops considerably), these contemporary apartments are a short distance from the castle. They have sleek kitchens, living rooms and views of the exclusive Park area. The two-bedroom apartments all have two bathrooms. ⓐ The Ropewalk ⓣ 0845 122 0405 ⓦ www.nottingham.sacoapartments.co.uk

THE BEST OF NOTTINGHAM

There's plenty to see in Nottingham, but luckily it's a compact city so you can easily reach most of the attractions on foot. Make sure you combine sightseeing with at least one lazy meal in one of the city's excellent restaurants.

TOP 10 ATTRACTIONS

- **Nottingham Castle** Perched on a rocky outcrop at the heart of the Norman city, this stately home is now a museum and art gallery (see page 70).

- **Nottingham Contemporary** Cutting-edge architecture and thought-provoking exhibitions at this excellent modern art gallery (see page 49).

- **City of Caves** Step inside some of the sandstone caves that lie beneath the city streets and discover Nottingham's hidden history (see page 67).

- **Bridlesmith Gate** Nottingham's best shopping street, lined with tempting clothes and shoe shops (see page 14).

- **Galleries of Justice Museum** Atmospheric, often spine-chilling, reminders of prison life and punishment in Nottingham's historic jail (see page 48).

- **St Barnabas Cathedral** This cathedral conceals an extraordinarily colourful chapel designed by the gothic revivalist Pugin (see page 67).

- **Nottingham Playhouse** Enjoy a drink or two beside Anish Kapoor's eye-catching *Sky Mirror* sculpture, before taking in a performance at the theatre (see page 78).

- **Sport on the Trent** The Trent is home to two football clubs, as well as Trent Bridge Cricket Ground. Get tickets for a match, or take a tour of the cricket ground (see page 20).

- **Ye Olde Trip to Jerusalem** This wonderfully atmospheric pub claims to be the oldest in England (see page 78).

- **Broad Street** This street in trendy Hockley is lined with lively bars, cafés and restaurants – a great place to eat (see page 17).

Snap up tickets for a match at Trent Bridge Cricket Ground

Suggested itineraries

HALF-DAY: A SPRINT ROUND THE CITY

If you've only got a few hours visit **Nottingham Castle** (see page 70), which has a museum and art gallery. On a fine day enjoy panoramic views from the castle's café terrace or picnic in the grounds. If you've time, head downhill to the **Museum of Nottingham Life at Brewhouse Yard Museum** (see page 69), close to the famous **Ye Olde Trip to Jerusalem** pub (see page 78).

1 DAY: A FULL DAY TO EXPLORE

Spend the morning at the castle, then have a leisurely lunch at one of the excellent restaurants nearby. Start the afternoon with a tour of Nottingham's fascinating cave system at **City of Caves** (see page 67). You should then have enough time to visit either **Nottingham Contemporary** (see page 49) or the **Galleries of Justice Museum** (see page 48), before making your way to the **Old Market Square** (see page 56). From here, it's just a short walk to the bars and restaurants of Chapel Bar or Broad Street.

2–3 DAYS: A LONG WEEKEND

With a bit more time, you should certainly add at least one of Nottingham's churches to your itinerary: **St Mary's Church** (see page 45), perhaps, for its stained glass, or **St Barnabas Cathedral** (see page 67) for its striking Pugin chapel. You should also stroll around the historic **Lace Market**, shop in Paul Smith's flagship store and have a leisurely afternoon tea at The Walk café. One evening you could take in a performance at the **Theatre Royal** (see page 66) or the **Nottingham Playhouse** (see page 78).

LONGER: OUT AND ABOUT

A longer stay would not only allow you to see all the city-centre sights – and shops – but would also allow you to visit attractions on the outskirts, like **Wollaton Hall** (see page 58). You could even hire a car and explore the surrounding countryside, perhaps venturing to **Newstead Abbey** (see page 83).

◆ Take a jaunt to Newstead Abbey and enjoy the gardens in spring

Something for nothing

Even if you're on a budget you'll find plenty to do in Nottingham. Art lovers will be pleased to hear that the city's excellent **Nottingham Contemporary** (see page 49) is free, as is the **Lakeside Arts Centre** (see page 69) at the University of Nottingham. Also free are the city's churches, in which you will find fine stained glass and carvings in stone, wood and alabaster.

The city's streets are a gallery in themselves – dotted with eye-catching buildings, notably those by eccentric architect Watson Fothergill. Make sure you wander through the **Lace Market** too, where former lace mills provide imposing reminders of Nottingham's industrial past.

You could easily spend hours window shopping, or watching the world go by in the Old Market Square. On fine days picnic in the **Arboretum** (see page 56) or go out to **Wollaton Hall** (see page 58), which has extensive grounds and a deer park – all free.

AN AWARD-WINNING UNIVERSITY

In 2000 the University of Nottingham became the first British university to open a campus in Malaysia – and one of the first to do so anywhere in the world. It now also boasts a campus in Ningbo, China, opened in 2005. In recognition of its achievement in forging strong international links, the university was awarded the Queen's Award for Enterprise in 2001 and later, in 2006, the Queen's Award for Industry.

When it rains

Like anywhere else in Britain, you can expect rain in Nottingham. That shouldn't spoil your visit though, as the city is well geared up with indoor attractions – and also has lots of bars and cafés where you can while away an hour or two.

Perhaps the best place to be on a rainy day is underground, so a tour of the man-made sandstone caves at **City of Caves** (see page 67) would be ideal. Discover the varied ways they have been used over the years; each use reflecting the wider history of the city itself. For those who like their culture, **Nottingham Contemporary** (see page 49) and **Bonington Art Gallery** (see page 60) are both a good bet, as is **Bromley House Library** (see page 60), a hidden gem of a property just off Old Market Square. Slightly outside the city centre, **Wollaton Hall** (see page 58) is home to Nottingham's **Natural History Museum** as well as the **Industrial Museum** (although the latter is only open one Sunday a month). In the heart of the city are the **Museum of Nottingham Life at Brewhouse Yard Museum** (see page 69) and the **Galleries of Justice Museum** (see page 48), where lashing rain beating down outside would only add to the atmosphere inside the grim Victorian prison cells.

Shoppers keen to exercise their credit cards will be pleased to know that Nottingham has three indoor shopping centres, the largest of which is the **Victoria Centre**. Those preferring to keep themselves active should don their skates and practise their moves on the Olympic-sized rinks at the **National Ice Centre** (see page 21). Who knows, maybe you could be another Jayne Torvill or Christopher Dean in the making?

On arrival

ARRIVING

By air

East Midlands Airport, Castle Donington, Derby (☎ 0871 919 9000 🌐 www.eastmidlandsairport.com) is situated just 21 km (13 miles) southwest of Nottingham. Its facilities include bars, restaurants, a bureau de change, car rental, shops, a prayer room and an executive lounge. There's also free Wi-Fi access. Flights go to destinations in the UK (including Aberdeen, Edinburgh and Glasgow), Ireland, the Channel Islands and Europe. In summer there are also direct flights to Newquay in Cornwall. Airlines operating from here include bmi, bmibaby, Ryanair and Thomsonfly.

There are good connections to and from Nottingham city centre. The Skylink bus (☎ 0115 950 6070 🌐 www.skylink.co.uk) runs every 30 minutes during the day, and hourly at night, 24 hours, daily. The journey takes 45 minutes and the bus drops passengers off at Friar Lane, very close to the Old Market Square. Alternatively, taxis are available at the airport – the journey costs around £30. They can be pre-booked from Arrow Cars (☎ 01332 814000 🌐 www.arrowprivatehire.co.uk).

Robin Hood Airport, near Doncaster (☎ 0871 220 2210 🌐 www.robinhoodairport.com) is situated just north of Nottinghamshire, in Yorkshire, about an hour's drive from Nottingham city centre. Flights go from here to European and long-haul destinations, including New York and Boston. Airlines operating from here include Aer Lingus, easyJet, Flybe and Ryanair.

This airport is less easy to reach by public transport. A shuttle service runs to Doncaster station, from where you can catch a train to Sheffield, where you must change again for Nottingham. Alternatively, the X30 bus goes to Worksop, which is served by direct trains to Nottingham.

By rail

Nottingham's railway station (ⓐ Station Street ⓣ 08457 48 49 50 ⓦ www.nationalrail.co.uk) is just ten minutes' walk from the Old Market Square. It is well served by trains from Manchester, Norwich, Leicester and Sheffield, with direct services also running to Matlock in the Peak District. There are good connections with Liverpool South Parkway (for John Lennon Airport) and Luton Airport Parkway. East Midlands Trains (ⓦ www.eastmidlandstrains.co.uk) operate frequent direct services to London St Pancras, where you can connect to Eurostar for trains to Paris and Brussels. The journey takes about 1 hour 45 minutes. There are plenty of taxis at Nottingham station, which is just five minutes' walk from Broadmarsh Bus Station.

By road

National Express coaches (ⓦ www.nationalexpress.com) run regular services between Nottingham (Broadmarsh Bus Station) and London Victoria Coach Station. The journey takes around 3 hours 30 minutes.

Nottingham is easily accessible by car as the M1 is just 9.6 km (6 miles) west of the city – junctions 24, 25 and 26 are closest to the city centre. The A1 runs to the east of the city and passes Sherwood Forest to the north. The A52 runs east/west

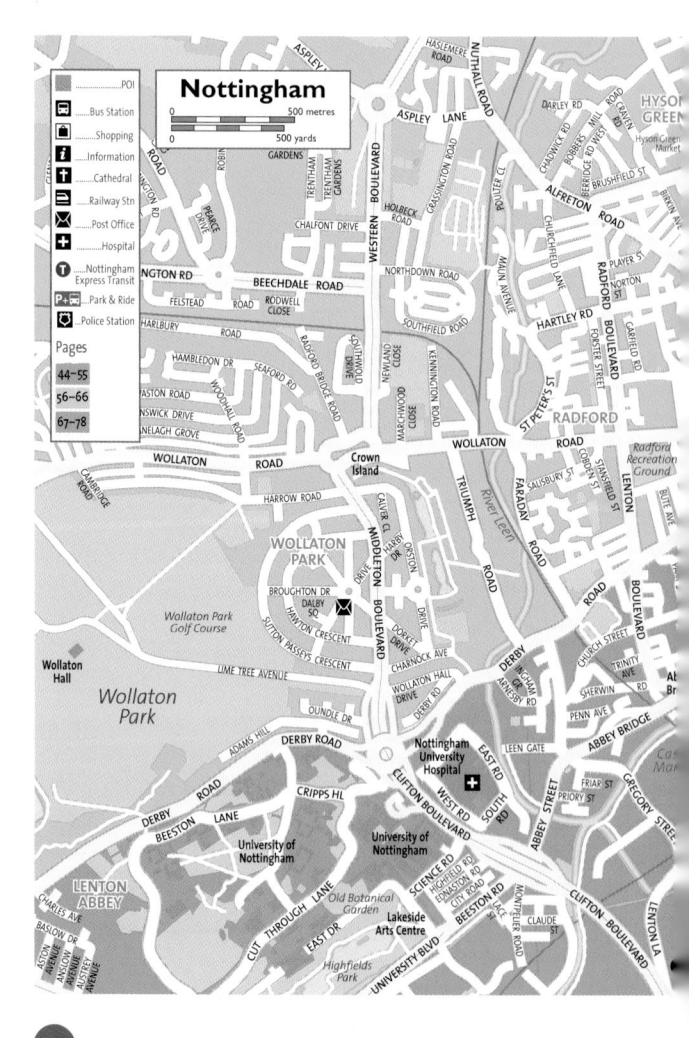

Nottingham

POI
Bus Station
Shopping
Information
Cathedral
Railway Stn
Post Office
Hospital
Nottingham Express Transit
Park & Ride
Police Station

Pages
44–55
56–66
67–78

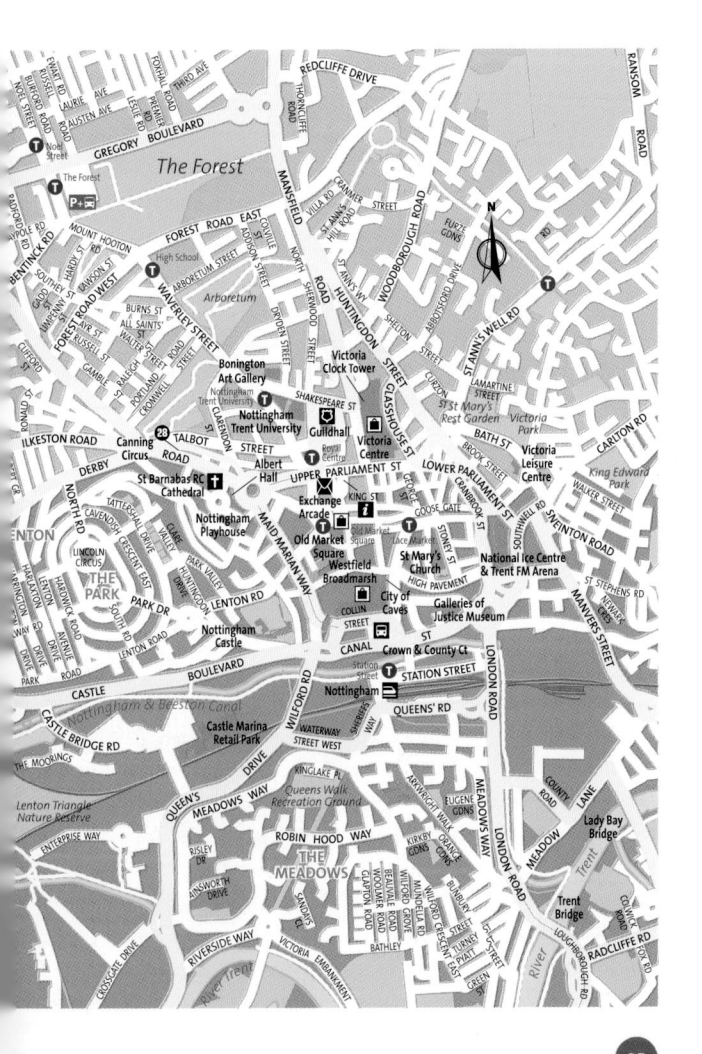

passing close to the city centre. Estimated drive times to the city are 40 minutes from the Peak District, 1 hour 50 minutes from Manchester, 1 hour 15 minutes from Birmingham and 2 hours 30 minutes from London. Much of the heart of Nottingham is pedestrianised. However, there are five NET park-and-ride spots around the city, all of which have free parking.

FINDING YOUR FEET

Nottingham is a small city and it's easy to get around on foot – many streets are pedestrianised. It's a lively, youthful city – not surprising as it has two universities – and can get a bit rowdy at night with groups of young people and stags/hens on pub crawls. However, the city centre generally feels safe (of course, you should take the usual sensible precautions). Although Nottingham has a reputation for higher than average crime rates, these have dropped significantly in recent years and trouble tends to be focused on outlying areas that are off the tourist trail.

ORIENTATION

Nottingham is pretty easy to navigate. The heart of the city is the Old Market Square (the dome of the Council House is a good central landmark) and the streets around it are pedestrianised. The main attractions and shopping areas are all within ten minutes' walk of the Square. Armed with one of the free maps from the Tourism Centre you shouldn't get lost.

GETTING AROUND

Nottingham has an excellent public transport system. The NET tram (ⓦ www.thetram.net) runs from Hucknall to the north of

⬥ *The station's building dates from the early 20th century*

the city centre, past Nottingham Trent University and the Old Market Square to the railway station. Payment can be made on board or at any outlet displaying the PayPoint sign. If you're planning to use the tram a lot then it's worth purchasing a carnet ten-trip ticket, or whichever is relevant of the one-, three- and seven-day tickets. The tram has links to a number of park-and-ride sites.

There are plenty of buses in Nottingham, run by both Nottingham City Transport (ⓦ www.nctx.co.uk) and Trent Barton (ⓦ www.trentbarton.co.uk), with services operating at night too. Tickets can be purchased on board – if you're doing more than one journey then it saves money to purchase an all day ticket. Kangaroo tickets allow unlimited travel for one day on buses, trains and trams with all operators in the city. Trent Barton's Indigo services run frequently and link the city centre with Queen Margaret's Hospital and the University of Nottingham. The main bus station is Broadmarsh.

Bike hire

Bicycles can be hired in **Clumber Park**, Worksop
(ⓣ 01909 544917 ⓦ www.nationaltrust.org.uk
ⓔ clumberpark@nationaltrust.org.uk)
and at **Sherwood Pines Centre** in Sherwood Forest
(ⓣ 01623 822 855 ⓦ www.sherwoodpinescycles.co.uk
ⓔ enquiries@sherwoodpinescycles.co.uk)

Car hire

It really isn't worth hiring a car if you're only planning to visit the city centre. However it could be a good idea if you want to

The NET tram route

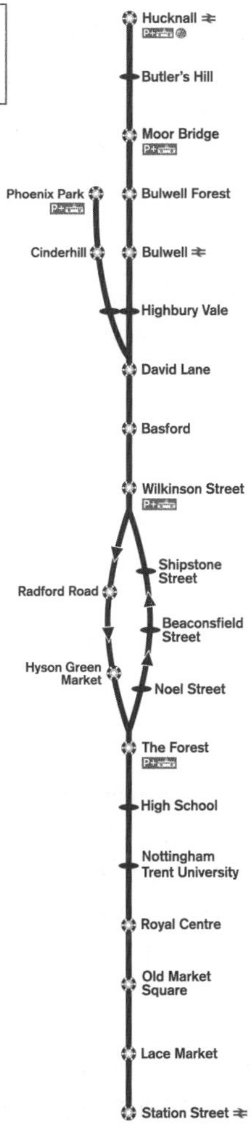

- Hucknall ≉
  P+ride ⊘
- Butler's Hill
- Moor Bridge
  P+ride
- Bulwell Forest
- Phoenix Park
  P+ride
- Cinderhill
- Bulwell ≉
- Highbury Vale
- David Lane
- Basford
- Wilkinson Street
  P+ride
- Shipstone Street
- Radford Road
- Beaconsfield Street
- Hyson Green Market
- Noel Street
- The Forest
  P+ride
- High School
- Nottingham Trent University
- Royal Centre
- Old Market Square
- Lace Market
- Station Street ≉

explore further afield and visit sights in the surrounding countryside.

Car rental is available with **Europcar** both at the airport and near the city centre at ⓐ Mabel Street ⓣ 0115 986 0308 ⓦ www.europcar.co.uk

Avis also have airport car hire and a city-centre location ⓐ The Arndale centre, Maid Marian Way ⓣ 0870 608 6354 ⓦ www.avis.com

East Mids Hire is on the outskirts of the city ⓐ Unit 1, Queens Court, Lenton Lane ⓣ 0115 985 2999 ⓦ www.eastmidshire.com

Taxis

Taxi ranks can be found throughout the city but the main ones are at the railway station and at Wheeler Gate, just off the Old Market Square.

DG Cars ⓣ 0115 9 607 607 ⓦ www.dgcars.co.uk

Trent Cars ⓣ 0115 9 50 50 50 ⓦ www.trentcars.com

▶ *Old meets new in this historic yet forward-looking city*

THE CITY OF
Nottingham

Introduction to city areas

Perched on high ground just north of the River Trent, Nottingham city centre is pleasantly compact. It can be readily divided into three distinct areas, making it easier for you to plan your stay.

In the east of the city centre are **Hockley** and the **Lace Market** – an area once famed for its lace factories and now revitalised as a hub for cool cafés and bars, and home to the city's contemporary art gallery.

The **Victoria** and **Royal** zones take in the heart of the city – the bustling Old Market Square, and most of the area to the north and northwest of that. They're a hub for shoppers and those seeking some night-time culture, and include the city's largest shopping mall, the Victoria Centre, and the Victorian Theatre Royal.

Finally, the **Castle** and **Canal** areas lie south and southwest of the Old Market Square and, as the names suggest, include Nottingham Castle as well as the city's main transport hubs – the railway and bus stations, and the canal.

Split between these last two zones are those attractions, such as Wollaton Park and the University of Nottingham, which lie slightly beyond the cluster of restaurants and churches that comprise the city's core.

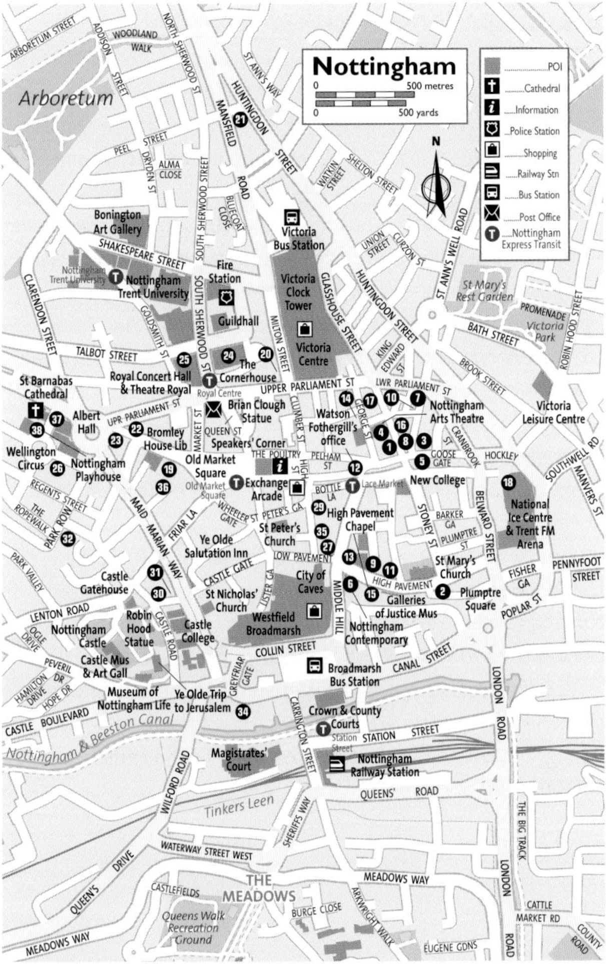
Nottingham
0
500 metres
0
500 yards
N
POI
Cathedral
Information
Police Station
Shopping
Railway Stn
Bus Station
Post Office
Nottingham Express Transit
Arboretum
ARBORETUM STREET
ADDISON STREET
WOODLAND WALK
NORTH SHERWOOD ST
ST ANN'S WAY
HUNTINGDON STREET
MANSFIELD ROAD
21
PEEL STREET
DRYDEN ST
ALMA CLOSE
SOUTH SHERWOOD STREET
BLUECOAT CLOSE
WATKIN STREET
SHELTON STREET
Bonington Art Gallery
Victoria Bus Station
UNION STREET
CURZON ST
ST ANN'S WELL ROAD
SHAKESPEARE STREET
Nottingham Trent University
Nottingham Trent University
Fire Station
Victoria Clock Tower
GLASSHOUSE STREET
HUNTINGDON STREET
St Mary's Rest Garden
CLARENDON STREET
GOLDSMITH ST
SOUTH SHERWOOD ST
Guildhall
Victoria Centre
PROMENADE
Victoria Park
ROBIN HOOD STREET
BATH STREET
TALBOT STREET
25
24
20
The Cornerhouse
MILTON STREET
KING EDWARD ST
BROOK STREET
St Barnabas Cathedral
Royal Concert Hall & Theatre Royal
Royal Centre
UPPER PARLIAMENT ST
LWR PARLIAMENT ST
14
17
10
7
Nottingham Arts Theatre
Victoria Leisure Centre
37
38
Albert Hall
UPR PARLIAMENT ST
Brian Clough Statue
MARKET ST
CLUMBER ST
Watson Fothergill's office
GEORGE ST
16
22
Bromley House Lib
23
QUEEN ST
Speakers' Corner
4
1
8
3
Wellington Circus
26
Nottingham Playhouse
Old Market Square
THE POULTRY
PELHAM ST
HIGH ST
12
5
GOOSE GATE
CRANBROOK ST
HOCKLEY
SOUTHWELL RD
MANVERS ST
19
36
Old Market Square
Exchange Arcade
BOTTLE LA
Lace Market
New College
18
REGENTS STREET
THE ROPEWALK
PARK ROW
MAID MARIAN WAY
FRIAR LA
WHEELER GATE
ST PETER'S GA
29
High Pavement Chapel
STONEY ST
BARKER GA
PLUMPTRE ST
BELWARD STREET
National Ice Centre & Trent FM Arena
32
Ye Olde Salutation Inn
St Peter's Church
35
27
PARK VALLEY
31
Castle Gatehouse
30
CASTLE GATE
LOW PAVEMENT
City of Caves
13
9
11
St Mary's Church
FISHER GA
PENNYFOOT STREET
St Nicholas' Church
LISTER GA
HIGH PAVEMENT
6
15
Galleries of Justice Mus
2
Plumptre Square
POPLAR ST
LENTON ROAD
Robin Hood Statue
CASTLE ROAD
Castle College
Westfield Broadmarsh
MIDDLE HILL
Nottingham Contemporary
OGLE DRIVE
Nottingham Castle
Castle Mus & Art Gall
COLLIN STREET
GREYFRIAR GATE
PEVERIL DR
Broadmarsh Bus Station
CANAL STREET
HAMILTON DRIVE
HOPE DR
Museum of Nottingham Life
Ye Olde Trip to Jerusalem
34
LONDON ROAD
CASTLE BOULEVARD
Crown & County Courts
Station Street
STATION STREET
CARRINGTON STREET
Nottingham & Beeston Canal
Magistrates' Court
Nottingham Railway Station
WILFORD ROAD
QUEENS' ROAD
Tinkers Leen
SHERIFFS WAY
THE BIG TRACK
WATERWAY STREET WEST
DRIVE
QUEEN'S
CASTLEFIELDS
THE MEADOWS
MEADOWS WAY
LONDON ROAD
Queens Walk Recreation Ground
BURGE CLOSE
ARKWRIGHT WALK
CATTLE MARKET RD
COUNTY ROAD
MEADOWS WAY
EUGENE GDNS

Lace Market & Hockley

As you stroll through the Lace Market zone, you're walking over the remains of Saxon Nottingham, the oldest part of the town. As the name suggests, it was the lace-making industry of the 19th century that really shaped this area and left a lasting architectural legacy. Former factories, such as those along Hollowstone and Plumptre Street, have now been converted into trendy flats and mingle with edgier modern buildings, such as the striking Nottingham Contemporary. To imagine what the city was like in its industrial heyday you need only to look up at the imposing warehouses that once powered the place to prosperity. Alternatively, opt for a free audio guide from the Galleries of Justice Museum – leave a deposit, pick up an MP3 player and wander through the streets as you find out all about the area's history.

Just north of the remaining factories you come into the Hockley area, where the streets take on a more bohemian character. Pelham Street and Goose Gate in particular are lined with independent shops, chilled cafés and bars. The best way to explore the whole area is on foot – just hop off the tram at Lace Market.

SIGHTS & ATTRACTIONS

High Pavement Chapel

Lovers of stained glass should pop into this former church, now converted into a branch of the Pitcher and Piano chain. A Unitarian chapel was first erected on this spot in the 17th century and later rebuilt in the 1870s. The church's soaring spire is one of the city's most notable landmarks and its windows are stunning. The finest of these is the great East Window, which was created by the Arts and Crafts firm Morris and Co (founded by William Morris) using designs by Burne-Jones. ⓐ 18 High Pavement Ⓝ Tram: Lace Market

St Mary's Church

This largely 15th-century building stands on a spot that has been occupied by a church since Saxon times. It's one of the finest medieval churches in England, on whose ancient stones

THE BIRTHPLACE OF BOOTS

There's a branch of Boots on practically every British high street, but this retailing giant had humble origins. In 1849 John and Mary Boot, who lived in the poor Hockley area of Nottingham, began selling herbal remedies from a small shop in Goose Gate. When John died in 1860, Mary kept the business going – and when her son Jesse left school a few years later at the age of 13, he joined her. In 1878, he leased a larger shop on Goose Gate with accommodation for staff on the top floor – the building is home to The Larder restaurant today. Jesse built up the business so successfully that he was knighted. By 1920 there were branches of Boots all over the country and he was able to sell the business for over £2 million. The company's headquarters are still in Nottingham.

◆ *The steps outside St Mary's Church*

GEORGE AFRICANUS

St Mary's graveyard is the burial site of Nottingham's first black entrepreneur, George Africanus (1763–1834). Brought to England as a child from Sierra Leone, before the abolition of slavery, he was a servant in a household in the Midlands. The family he served was liberal by inclination and he was educated and later apprenticed as a brass founder. He moved to Nottingham and married a local girl, with whom he then started a business.

multiple generations have made their mark. There are fascinating reminders of Nottingham's industrial heritage to be seen, along with some examples of rare Nottingham alabaster. One piece, now protected by a glass panel, was found during restoration work buried face down beneath the church floor. ⓐ High Pavement ⓣ 0115 948 3658 ⓦ www.nottinghamchurches.org ⓛ Open for visitors 10.00–15.00 Tues–Sat ⓝ Tram: Lace Market

Watson Fothergill's office

As you stroll around Nottingham you can't fail to be struck by the large number of fine brick buildings in the city. The most eye-catching of all is this flamboyant building on George Street. It was designed by Nottingham's best-known architect Watson Fothergill (1841–1928), whose distinctive and eccentric style can be seen throughout the city. He let his creative instincts run wild in particular on this, his own office, which is adorned with an

● *Be sure to be on your best behaviour at the Galleries of Justice Museum*

exuberant flurry of stone carvings, friezes, arches and pillars.
It isn't open to the public. ⓐ 15 George Street
Ⓝ Tram: Lace Market

CULTURE

Galleries of Justice Museum

The elegant neo-classical frontage of Nottingham's Shire Hall
conceals an interior that tells far darker tales. The city's former
courtrooms and county jail have been turned into an
atmospheric museum devoted to tales of crime and
punishment. Hold the chains that once shackled prisoners
to the wall and see the medieval oubliette – an almost

inaccessible dungeon into which prisoners were flung and then forgotten. ⓐ High Pavement ⓣ 0115 952 0555 ⓦ www.galleriesofjustice.org.uk ⓒ 10.00–17.00 daily; performance tours Wed–Sun; self-guided audio tours Mon & Tues ⓝ Tram: Lace Market ⓘ Admission charge

Nottingham Contemporary

Contemporary art was given a striking new home in 2009 when this edgy new gallery opened. It may look unwelcoming from the outside, but inside it's airy and light with galleries that play host to changing exhibitions of contemporary art – generally accompanied by a programme of lively talks, discussions and special events. Be aware that the gallery space closes for a short time between exhibitions, but the shop and café are always open. ⓐ Weekday Cross ⓣ 0115 948 9750 ⓦ www.nottinghamcontemporary.org ⓒ 10.00–19.00 Tues–Fri, 10.00–18.00 Sat & bank holidays, 11.00–17.00 Sun ⓝ Tram: Lace Market

RETAIL THERAPY

Cashé This shop specialises in designer childrenswear, so it's the place to come if you want Dior, Diesel or Dolce and Gabbana for the children. ⓐ 42 Pelham Street ⓣ 0115 941 1617 ⓦ www.cashenottingham.co.uk

Kitsch Fans of vintage will love this shop, which stocks a wide range of retro clothes, shoes and boots. ⓐ 19–21 Pelham Street ⓣ 0115 924 2353

Michael Levin If you're looking for some classy jewellery with a difference, seek out this discreet little jeweller and diamond merchant on Pelham Street. As well as stocking antique items, it also sells loose diamonds. There's a working goldsmith on the premises, so you can select your stones, then get them set in a design of your choosing. ⓐ 25 Pelham Street
ⓣ 0115 941 8600

Projects Brand-conscious men and women will find plenty of trendy labels in this shop. Names range from Hugo Boss and Miss Sixty, to more rock 'n' roll brands like Religion and Buddhist Punk. ⓐ 32 Pelham Street ⓣ 0115 956 7005
ⓦ www.projectsclothing.com

ⓐ *Nottingham Contemporary's modern exterior*

TAKING A BREAK

Edin's £ ❶ Edin's is a Nottingham institution, functioning as a café/wine bar and offering everything from breakfast in the mornings to tapas, and more substantial bistro-style dishes such as baked goat's cheese focaccia. It also offers a selection of cakes and has free Wi-Fi. ⓐ 15 Broad Street ⓣ 0115 924 1112 ⓛ 08.00–24.00 Mon–Sat, 09.00–19.00 Sun

The Hungry Pumpkin £ ❷ Great little deli/café, opposite St Mary's Church in the Lace Market. Come for gourmet sandwiches (roast beef and homemade chutney, or maybe grape and brie), paninis, baked potatoes, all-day breakfasts and homemade cakes. ⓐ 38 High Pavement ⓣ 0115 948 0333 ⓦ www.hungrypumpkin.co.uk ⓛ 08.00–15.30 Mon–Fri, 09.30–17.00 Sat, 11.00–16.00 Sun

Jam Café £ ❸ There's a bohemian feel to this Hockley café, which offers an eclectic choice of dishes ranging from snacks like cheese on toast to more substantial fare such as scallop risotto. There's live music on Wed, Fri & Sat evenings. ⓐ 12 Heathcoat Street ⓣ 0115 948 3566 ⓛ 10.00–17.30 Mon & Tues, 10.00–24.00 Wed–Sat (food served until 21.30), 11.00–16.30 Sun

Lee Rosy's £ ❹ This earthy little café has a lovely relaxed atmosphere and offers a wide variety of teas as well as a selection of cakes and cheesecakes. Wheat-free treats are often available. ⓐ 17 Broad Street ⓦ www.lee-rosy.co.uk ⓛ 09.30–20.00 Mon & Tues, 10.00–22.00 Sat, 11.00–19.00 Sun

The Larder £–££ ❺ Although it's situated in the historic original Boots store, this excellent restaurant has a thoroughly contemporary feel. Dishes are imaginative but unfussy and the set lunches and early evening menus are great value.
ⓐ 1st Floor, 16–22 Goosegate ⓣ 0115 950 0111
ⓦ www.thelarderongoosegate.co.uk ⓛ 12.00–14.00 & 18.00–22.00 Tues–Sat, 12.00–15.00 Sun

Nottingham Contemporary Café £–££ ❻ One of Nottingham's coolest venues, this café in the contemporary art gallery offers a suitably modern take on classic British dishes such as fish and chips, bubble and squeak and even the knickerbocker glory. ⓐ Weekday Cross ⓣ 0115 948 9754
ⓦ www.cafebarcontemporary.com ⓛ 10.00–21.00 Tues & Wed, 10.00–23.00 Thur–Sat, 10.00–19.00 Sun

⬤ The Larder is renowned for putting British produce on the menu

Benton's Brasserie ££ ❼ This stylish, light and airy brasserie has a menu that changes with the seasons. Dishes might include chargrilled steak with stilton or pan-fried chicken with Cajun rice. Puddings meanwhile are indulgent – lime and ginger cheesecake perhaps, or sticky toffee pudding with butterscotch sauce. ⓐ 38 Heathcoat Street ⓣ 0115 959 9800 ⓦ www.bentonsbrasserie.co.uk ⓛ 12.00–14.30 & 18.00–23.00 Mon–Thur, 12.00–24.00 Fri & Sat, 12.00–15.45 Sun

Kayal ££ ❽ This noteworthy Indian restaurant specialises in the cuisine of Kerala. The menu offers a variety of dosas (filled pancakes made from soaked lentils and rice) and plenty of fish dishes. ⓐ 8 Broad Street ⓣ 0115 941 4733 ⓦ www.kayalrestaurant.com ⓛ 12.00–15.00 & 18.00–23.00 Mon–Fri, 12.00–23.00 Sat, 12.00–22.00 Sun

The Living Room ££ ❾ Situated in a former lace showroom, this bar/restaurant has an extensive menu offering light bites and plates of antipasti for sharing, as well as more substantial dishes like Gloucester Old Spot bangers with mash. Main meals are usually served until early evening. ⓐ 7 High Pavement ⓣ 0115 988 6870 ⓦ www.thelivingroom.co.uk ⓛ 12.00–24.00 Mon & Tues, 12.00–01.00 Wed & Thur, 12.00–02.00 Sat, 12.00–24.00 Sun

Squeek ££ ❿ Vegetarians and vegans will think they've gone to heaven at this restaurant which serves imaginative dishes that should please even the most dedicated meat-eater. The menu, which changes regularly, is divine. ⓐ 23–25 Heathcoat Street ⓣ 0115 955 5560 ⓛ 18.00–late Tues–Sat

Merchants £££ ⑪ Part of the Lace Market Hotel, this is one of Nottingham's finest restaurants. The interior is all dark wood and red leather, and the menu is largely meaty – lots of dishes featuring wood pigeon, pheasant and partridge and even a sophisticated version of that old English favourite, faggots. Tempting desserts might include roasted banana and passion fruit soufflé. ⓐ 29–31 High Pavement ⓣ 0115 852 3232 ⓦ www.thefinessecollection.com/lacemarket ⓛ 12.00–14.00 & 18.00–22.00 Tues–Fri, 18.00–22.00 Sat

AFTER DARK

PUBS, BARS & CLUBS

Bodega ⑫ This Hockley hangout has regular club nights and is also a live music venue – bands such as the Arctic Monkeys, Franz Ferdinand and the Scissor Sisters have all played here. ⓐ 23 Pelham Street ⓣ 0115 950 5078 ⓦ thebodegasocialclub.co.uk

Brass Monkey ⑬ Nottingham's first cocktail bar, this funky monkey in the Lace Market is the place to come for mojitos, martinis and margaritas. ⓐ 11 High Pavement ⓣ 0115 840 4101 ⓦ www.brassmonkeybar.co.uk

Coco Lounge Club ⑭ A large palm tree, squashy sofas and a smartly dressed crowd make Coco Lounge one of the most popular city clubs. ⓐ 3 George Street ⓣ 0115 941 8555 ⓛ 20.00–03.00 Mon–Sat

Pitcher and Piano ⓯ The soaring ceiling and stained-glass windows of this former church add a touch of ecclesiastical theatre to a night out. Come for drinks and dancing. ⓐ 18 High Pavement ⓣ 0115 958 6081 ⓦ www.pitcherandpiano.com ⓛ 12.00–24.00 Sun, Mon & Wed, 12.00–01.00 Tues & Thur, 12.00–02.00 Fri & Sat

ENTERTAINMENT
Broadway Cinema ⓰ This cinema screens everything from the latest Hollywood blockbusters to foreign films with subtitles. The **café/bar** is very popular too – food served 09.00–21.00 Mon–Sat, 10.00–21.00 Sun. ⓐ 14–18 Broad Street ⓣ 0115 952 6611 ⓦ www.broadway.org.uk

The Screenroom ⓱ It claims to be the world's smallest cinema, and with just 21 seats it might well be right. Not surprisingly, booking is advised. ⓐ 25b Broad Street ⓣ 0115 924 1133 ⓦ www.screenroom.co.uk

Trent FM Arena ⓲ The city's largest entertainment, sporting and conference venue, Trent FM regularly plays host to big names in the music industry – think Status Quo, Elton John, Michael Bublé – as well as comedy stars, Cirque du Soleil and other performers. ⓐ Bolero Square ⓣ 0844 124 624 (tickets) ⓦ www.trentfmarenanottingham.com

Victoria & Royal zones

In the zones, the focus of which is the large Old Market Square, you'll find the city's largest shopping centre as well as its fascinating historic independent library. The area is also home to one of Nottingham's most photographed sights – the statue of Brian Clough, which stands near the junction of King Street and Queen Street. Appropriately, given the charismatic football manager's gift for straight talking, the area beside the statue has been officially designated 'Speaker's Corner'.

SIGHTS & ATTRACTIONS

Arboretum

Nottingham's oldest public park, the Arboretum was opened in 1852 with the aim of providing a green space close to the city. Over 1,000 rare trees and shrubs were planted – there are still about 800 today – and it is now Grade II listed. As well as unusual trees like Ginkgo biloba, the Indian bean and the Tulip tree, the park has a Victorian aviary and a Chinese Bell Tower. Come for a walk or a picnic. ⓐ Waverley Street ⓝ Tram: Nottingham Trent University or High School

Old Market Square

The largest remaining medieval town square in England, the Old Market Square has long been a focus of Nottingham city life. A marketplace by the mid-12th century, it lay between the walled Norman town to the west and the Saxon town to the east, serving both communities. Over the centuries the square has

🔺 *The silver-tongued Brian Clough is honoured at Speaker's Corner*

been redesigned a number of times, most recently in 2007 by the architects who designed the Diana Memorial Fountain in London. The line of the original wall that divided Norman from Saxon Nottingham is picked out in a line of granite, while a giant water feature makes a popular paddling spot on hot days. At one end of the square is the neo-classical grandeur of the Council House, the city's main civic building. Ⓝ Tram: Old Market Square

Victoria Clock Tower

Looking rather incongruous against the concrete 1960s bulk of the Victoria Centre is this late-Victorian brick clock tower. Built in baroque style, it's a remnant of Nottingham's Victoria railway station, which was demolished to make way for the centre.

Wollaton Hall and Park

You could easily spend the whole day exploring this extravagant Elizabethan mansion and surrounding parkland,

THE GOOSE FAIR

The unusual name of this annual funfair is popularly thought to refer to the historical tradition of a goose sale, when thousands of geese would be driven to market in Nottingham from the surrounding counties. It gradually evolved into a general fair and food festival, taking over the town centre and lasting eight days. It took place each September until the calendar was altered in the 18th century, and is now held in October.

situated on the outskirts of the Royal zone. Wollaton Hall was built by Robert Smythson in the mid-16th century for the wealthy industrialist Sir Francis Willoughby, who owned coal mines in Nottinghamshire. Although damaged by fire in the 17th century and altered and restored a number of times throughout its history, it still retains many Elizabethan features. It is also home to the city's **Natural History Museum**, which has an array of stuffed animals and displays devoted to extinct and nearly extinct species. The former stables contain an **Industrial Museum** (only open one Sunday a month), which houses a fascinating array of items from steam engines to bicycles, as well as several important examples of Nottingham lace machinery.

🔺 *The impressive grounds of Wollaton Park are perfect for a picnic on a fine day*

The parkland, which is home to both red and fallow deer, covers 200 hectares (500 acres) and makes a great place for picnics. There are formal gardens with a fine Victorian glasshouse and a lake. ⓐ Wollaton, entrances on Derby Road and Wollaton Road ⓣ 0115 915 3900 ⓦ www.nottinghamcity.gov.uk ⓛ Hall and Museum 11.00–17.00 daily (Apr–Oct); 11.00–16.00 daily (Nov–Mar). Park 08.00–dusk Mon–Fri, 09.00–dusk Sat & Sun. Tours of the Hall 11.30 & 14.30 Mon–Fri, 11.30, 14.30 & 15.30 Sat & Sun ⓝ Bus: 30

CULTURE

Bonington Art Gallery

Nottingham Trent University's School of Art and Design holds exhibitions several times each year at this gallery. Work shown might be that of national and international artists, as well as that of students and staff. Well worth catching is the annual exhibition of work from final-year students: it showcases everything from fine art and photography to fashion and knitwear. ⓐ Bonington Building, Dryden Street ⓣ 0115 848 8327 ⓦ www.ntu.ac.uk ⓝ Tram: Nottingham Trent University

Bromley House Library

This fine 18th-century townhouse is hard to spot, with a hidden entrance that gives no hint of what's inside. Yet the subscription library it houses is a real gem and well worth visiting: a succession of book-lined rooms with ornate fireplaces, decorative plaster ceilings and wood panelling –

you half expect to find Dr Johnson sitting in a corner working on his dictionary. One room, accessed by a spiral staircase, has a brass meridian line running along the floor, which is hit by the sun, from a peephole in the window, at noon. Although the library is only open to members, it runs monthly tours.
ⓐ Angel Row ⓣ 0115 947 3134 ⓦ www.bromleyhouse.org
ⓝ Tram: Old Market Square ⓘ Small charge for bookable tours. Phone in advance

RETAIL THERAPY

The Cheese Shop With over 200 different cheeses to choose from, you should find something here to tickle your taste buds. Look out for cheeses from the Midlands, such as Lincolnshire Poacher. ⓐ FH Mall, The Poultry ⓣ 0115 941 9114

The Clock Emporium Antique clocks and watches on sale, with specialists able to carry out repairs too. ⓐ 115 Mansfield Road ⓣ 0115 947 6228

Daphne's Handbag Vintage and retro items galore, with clothes, jewellery and homeware to choose from. ⓐ 67 Mansfield Road ⓣ 0115 924 0550

Dave Mann Music Specialist music shop with a wide range of guitars, as well as violins and other stringed instruments. Knowledgeable staff and an in-house luthier who can carry out repairs. ⓐ 123–125 Mansfield Road ⓣ 0115 941 7955
ⓦ www.davemann.co.uk

Good Vibrations Second-hand record shop with a selection of vinyl and CDs. ⓐ 149 Mansfield Road ⓣ 0115 941 1663

Jermy and Westerman Specialist antiquarian bookseller, with a good choice of out-of-print books. ⓐ 203 Mansfield Road ⓣ 0115 947 4522

Kathleen and Lily's Vintage and customised clothing, jewellery and handmade gifts and accessories. ⓐ 205 Mansfield Road ⓣ 0115 941 2327 ⓦ www.kathleenandlilys.co.uk

Shawes Art Shop Excellent selection of artists' supplies, ranging from easels to paints and pencils. ⓐ 68–70 Mansfield Road ⓣ 0115 941 8646 ⓦ www.shawes.co.uk

Vivienne Westwood The grande dame of edgy fashion, Vivienne Westwood has accessories, shoes and perfume as well as clothes that make a statement. ⓐ FH Mall, The Poultry ⓣ 0115 941 7300 ⓦ www.hervia.com

TAKING A BREAK

The Bell Inn £ ⓳ This pub just off the Old Market Square dates back to the 15th century and vies for the title of Nottingham's oldest pub with the Salutation and Ye Olde Trip to Jerusalem (see page 78). It's a great place to stop for a lunchtime sandwich or a more substantial traditional pub meal. Vegetarian choices are also good and include a mushroom suet pudding and a Red Leicester and spinach burger. Sunday lunches with all the

trimmings are very popular. ⓐ 18 Angel Row ⓣ 0115 947 5241
ⓛ Food served daily 12.00–21.00

Le Bistrot Pierre £–££ ⓴ As the name suggests, French cuisine is
on the menu at this central restaurant, housed in a former bank,
which offers good value set lunches and pre-theatre meals.
Dishes include starters like brioche filled with mushrooms, and
mains such as steaks, sharing plates and classics like beef
bourguignon. Twice a month there's a gastronomic evening
featuring a six-course set menu – unusually for a French
restaurant there's even an alternative vegetarian menu.
ⓐ 13–17 Milton Street ⓣ 0115 941 2850
ⓦ www.lebistrotpierre.co.uk ⓛ Lunch 12.00–15.00 Mon–Sat,
12.30–15.30 Sun; dinner 17.30–22.00 Mon, 17.30–22.30 Tues–Thur,
17.30–23.00 Fri & Sat, 18.00–22.00 Sun

Nagoyaka £–££ ㉑ Japanese and Korean dishes are on the menu
here, with sushi, sashimi, kimchi and dishes like Gyu Kare Rice
(stir-fried beef and vegetables with curry sauce) and Ika Daikon
(braised squid). Those who like to experiment might wish to try
the 'Fried Mixed Bacterio'. ⓐ 148 Mansfield Road ⓣ 0115 950 3333
ⓛ 12.00–15.00 & 17.00–23.00 daily

Sinatras ££ ㉒ You've a chance of doing some celebrity spotting
at this popular Chapel Bar restaurant – Gordon Ramsay and
Midge Ure have both been seen here (though not together!).
The large menu changes regularly but generally features pasta
dishes, risottos and dishes from around the world like lamb
tagine and prawn curry. Go for rum and raisin cheesecake or

chocolate tart for pudding. They do a popular Sunday lunch too.
🅐 8–16 Chapel Bar 🕐 0115 941 1050
🅦 www.sinatrarestaurant.com 🕐 10.00–23.00 Mon–Thur (last food orders 21.30), 10.00–24.00 Fri & Sat (last food orders 22.00), 10.00–22.30 Sun (last food orders 21.00)

Tonic ££ ㉓ Shiny wood, glowing red lights and uncluttered retro chic make for a relaxed atmosphere at this restaurant in the city centre whose food has earned an AA rosette. Fresh local produce features on the regularly changing menu, which specialises in modern British cuisine with dishes like pan-fried sea trout or shoulder of Derbyshire lamb, and plenty of choice for vegetarians. Some quirky desserts are offered like Irn Bru sorbet or tonka bean panacotta. 🅐 6 Chapel Bar 🕐 0115 941 4770 🅦 www.tonic-online.co.uk 🕐 Restaurant 12.00–14.00 & 18.00–22.00 daily; bar food 10.00–19.00 Mon–Fri, 10.00–18.00 Sat & Sun

Saltwater ££–£££ ㉔ Situated on the rooftop of the rather unenticing looking Cornerhouse development, Saltwater serves up modern British cuisine along with some fine views of the city. The menu changes with the seasons, but you might find dishes like slow-cooked lamb shank or pan-fried duck with bubble and squeak, as well as tempting vegetarian dishes like asparagus, pecorino and broad bean risotto.
🅐 The Cornerhouse, Forman Street 🕐 0115 924 2664
🅦 www.saltwater-restaurant.com 🕐 Restaurant: 12.00–14.30 & 17.30–22.00 Mon–Thur, 12.00–15.00 & 17.30–22.30 Fri & Sat

AFTER DARK

PUBS, BARS & CLUBS

In addition to the popular Bell Inn on Angel Row (see page 62), there are a number of pubs worth checking out on the Mansfield Road. The **Lincolnshire Poacher** (ⓐ 161–163 Mansfield Road ⓣ 0115 941 1584) has good beer and pub food; the **Golden Fleece** (ⓐ 105 Mansfield Road ⓣ 0115 947 2843) serves up live music, real ales and great homemade food, and also boasts a roof terrace, and the **Peacock** (ⓐ 11 Mansfield Road ⓣ 0115 947 2152) has decent real ales. Also popular is **Saltwater** (see opposite), which doubles as a slick bar. Enjoy spectacular views over the city from the stylish rooftop terrace.

🔺 *Saltwater restaurant in the Cornerhouse*

ENTERTAINMENT

Theatre Royal and Royal Concert Hall ㉕ The Victorian Theatre Royal has a great programme of plays (often direct from London's West End), operas and ballets – as well as Christmas pantomimes. Part of the same complex is the late 20th-century Royal Concert Hall, which hosts musicals, dance performances and some classical concerts. ⓐ Theatre Square ⓣ 0115 989 5555 ⓦ www.royalcentre-nottingham.co.uk ⓝ Tram: Royal Centre

🔺 *Top-class entertainment at the Theatre Royal*

Castle zone & Canal

You can really dip your toes into Nottingham's past in this area, which was the heart of the Norman town which grew up in the shadow of the castle. There are several historic churches, some exclusive Georgian and Victorian streets, and a hidden honeycomb of caves which snakes beneath the city streets. This area is also where you'll find some of Nottingham's finest restaurants and its best shopping street.

SIGHTS & ATTRACTIONS

City of Caves

Of all Nottingham's sights, this is surely the most unexpected and most interesting. From the decidedly modern surroundings of the Westfield Broadmarsh, you step into some of the caves that underpin the city. These man-made structures dug into the soft sandstone date from Saxon times. Over the centuries they've had a variety of uses as cellars, prisons, homes and air-raid shelters. Visit the remains of a 16th- and 17th-century tannery and the cave that was a pub cellar where highwaymen were known to hide out. ❸ Upper Level, Westfield Broadmarsh ❶ 0115 988 1955 Ⓦ www.cityofcaves.com ◷ 10.30–17.00 daily (last admission 16.00) Ⓝ Tram: Lace Market ❶ Admission charge

St Barnabas Cathedral

Built in 1844, this Catholic cathedral is one of Nottingham's real gems. It was designed by A W N Pugin, the Victorian architect who spearheaded the Gothic Revival and is best known for the interiors of the Palace of Westminster in London. The cathedral's highlight is the Blessed Sacrament Chapel, a brilliantly coloured confection of scarlet, gold and green. ⓐ Derby Road ⓣ 0115 953 9839 ⓦ www.stbarnabascathedral.org.uk

🔺 *Journey back in time in the remarkable City of Caves*

St Nicholas' Church

St Nicholas dates back to the 12th century, but the church you see today was built in the 17th. The tower of the earlier building was used by Royalist forces to fire at Parliamentarians in the nearby castle. Parliamentary troops retaliated by destroying the church. @ Maid Marian Way ☏ 0115 952 4600

St Peter's Church

There has been a church on this site since Norman times, though the current building is essentially medieval. Used during the Civil War as a sanctuary for Royalist troops, the church was partly destroyed by Parliamentary forces. Inside you'll see an array of stone carvings, of which one is thought to be medieval. The wooden cover for the font was carved by Robert Thompson, a Yorkshireman famed for his trademark mouse. @ St Peter's Gate ☏ 0115 948 3658 ⓦ www.nottinghamchurches.org ⏱ 10.00–16.00 Mon–Sat, closed Sun

CULTURE

Lakeside Arts Centre

Set beside the lake on the main University of Nottingham campus, this arts centre offers a lively programme of exhibitions and performances. @ University Park, University of Nottingham ☏ 0115 951 4764 ⓦ www.lakesidearts.org.uk Ⓝ Bus: 13, 14

Museum of Nottingham Life at Brewhouse Yard Museum

Set in a terrace of 17th-century cottages beneath the castle rock, this museum of Nottingham's past comprises reconstructed rooms, including a Victorian schoolroom and a kitchen, old shop frontages and displays of toys. Part of the exhibition is set into sandstone caves, filled with reminders of wartime Nottingham.

ⓐ Brewhouse Yard, Castle Boulevard ❶ 0115 915 3640

ⓦ www.nottinghamcity.gov.uk ❶ 10.00–16.30 Tues–Sun

Ⓝ Bus: 13, 14 ❶ Admission charge

Nottingham Castle

A statue of Robin Hood stands outside the walls of Nottingham Castle, a reminder that this was once the home of his legendary arch-enemy, the Sheriff of Nottingham. The Normans first built a

● *The castle now houses an impressive art gallery*

castle on this rocky outcrop in 1067 and it later became one of the most important royal castles in England. Richard III stayed here before the Battle of Bosworth, and in 1642 Charles I raised his standard outside the walls, to rally his troops at the start of the Civil War. Little remains today except the gatehouse (the castle's history has been as turbulent as England's own). The mansion that rose in its place suffered heavy damage in early 19th-century political riots, but has since been restored. Now the building is a museum and art gallery, with exhibitions inside relating to Nottingham's history and works by artists such as Dante Gabriel Rossetti and L S Lowry. The castle is built upon a series of man-made caves, used variously as prison cells and wine cellars, and if you're up to negotiating the 300 steps, it's worth joining one of the regular tours. The grounds cover 2.4 hectares (6 acres) and make a great picnic spot, while the café offers superb panoramic views of the city and surrounding countryside. ⓐ Friar Lane/Castle Gate ⓣ 0115 915 3700 ⓦ www.nottinghamcity.gov.uk ⓛ 10.00–16.00 Tues–Sun (Oct–Feb); 10.00–17.00 Tues–Sun (Mar–Sept) ⓝ Bus: 13, 14 ⓘ Admission charge

RETAIL THERAPY

Celia's Vintage Clothing Whether you want a 1930s nightdress or a pair of 1960s flares, this vintage clothes store should have it. It also sells fancy dress. ⓐ 66–68 Derby Road ⓣ 0115 947 3036 ⓦ www.celias-nottm.co.uk ⓛ 10.00–17.00 Mon–Sat, closed Sun

Le Chien et Moi This lovely shop stocks a tempting mix of gifts and homeware – it's shabby chic meets Homes and Gardens.

Inside you'll find vintage and new furniture as well as candles, clocks and ceramics. ⓐ 60 Derby Road ⓣ 0115 979 9199 ⓦ www.lechienetmoi.com ⓛ 10.30–17.30 Tues–Sat, closed Sun & Mon

Joe's Store An eclectic mix of gifts here, with everything from Tintin merchandise to Orla Kiely bags and some items for the home. ⓐ 61 Friar Lane ⓣ 07973 764220 or 0115 941 8882 ⓦ www.joesstore.co.uk ⓝ Tram: Old Market Square

M Kemp Antiques Family-owned antique dealers specialising in silver and gold jewellery. ⓐ 79–81 Derby Road ⓣ 0115 837 9495 ⓛ 10.00–17.00 Mon–Wed, Fri & Sat

▲ *Victorian Nottingham at Brewhouse Yard Museum (see pages 69–70)*

Nottingham Society of Artists This gallery/shop exhibits the work of members of the Nottingham Society of Artists. It's a good place to browse and you can find paintings, ceramics and sculptures for sale. 🅰 71–73 Friar Lane ☎ 0115 948 0476 🔼 www.nottinghamartists.org.uk 🕐 10.00–16.30 daily 🚊 Tram: Old Market Square

Paul Smith The Nottingham-born designer's flagship store is in Willoughby House, one of the city's finest 18th-century properties. It stocks men's and women's clothes and accessories, while his Byard Lane shop specialises in jeans and shoes. 🅰 Willoughby House, 20 Low Pavement ☎ 0115 968 5990; 🅰 10 Byard Lane ☎ 0115 950 6712 🔼 www.paulsmith.co.uk 🕐 10.00–18.00 Mon–Sat, 12.00–16.00 Sun 🚊 Tram: Old Market Square

Weavers of Nottingham Established since 1844, this family-owned wine merchant has an excellent range of wines and spirits. You can find everything from fine champagne to Lebanese wines, as well as over 140 single malt whiskies, unusual liqueurs and even 'Robin Hood' mead. 🅰 1 Castle Gate ☎ 0115 958 0922 🔼 www.weaverswines.com

TAKING A BREAK

CAST Restaurant and Deli £ 26 Whether you want a pre-theatre meal or a lunchtime sandwich, this restaurant and deli adjacent to Nottingham Playhouse has a large outdoor seating area and is definitely worth checking out. As well as pasta dishes it has sharing plates, bread and olives, and more substantial dishes such as salmon and crab fish cakes. **ⓐ** Wellington Circus **ⓣ** 0115 852 3898 **ⓦ** www.castrestaurant.co.uk **ⓛ** 12.00–22.00 Mon–Sat, 12.00–18.00 Sun

Delilah £ ㉗ Award-winning deli with a great choice of cheeses, salamis, meats and other treats – ideal if you want to put together a picnic. It also functions as a relaxed café, serving tapas-style dishes. **ⓐ** 15 Middle Pavement **ⓣ** 0115 948 4461 **ⓦ** www.delilahfinefoods.co.uk **ⓛ** 08.00–19.00 Mon–Fri, 09.00–19.00 Sat, 11.00–17.00 Sun

The Sir John Borlase Warren £ ㉘ Refurbished Victorian pub with squashy sofas and a courtyard garden. Soups, sandwiches and salads are served for lunch and more substantial meals in the evening such as fish pie, surf and turf, or salmon with samphire. **ⓐ** 1 Ilkeston Road, Canning Circus **ⓣ** 0115 947 4247 **ⓛ** Food: 12.00–15.00 & 17.00–22.00 Mon–Fri, 12.00–22.00 Sat, 12.00–15.00 & 17.00–20.00 Sun **ⓝ** Bus: 28, 34, 77

The Walk Café £–££ ㉙ Don't miss this lovely café that is tucked away down the Bridlesmith Walk passageway, which leads off Bridlesmith Gate. A world of gilded mirrors, modern artworks and funky mismatched china, the café serves delicious open sandwiches and salads, but is best known for its gorgeous cakes. Treat yourself to afternoon tea, a feast of sandwiches (crusts cut off, of course), savouries and a selection of pastries. **ⓐ** 12 Bridlesmith Walk **ⓣ** 0115 947 7574 **ⓦ** www.thewalkcafe.co.uk **ⓛ** 08.00–20.00 Mon–Sat, 10.00–18.00 Sun **ⓝ** Tram: Lace Market

Fothergill's ££ ⑩ One of the city's newest restaurants, Fothergill's has a prime position by the castle with large windows looking over to the statue of Robin Hood. Come for sausages and mash, fish and chips, or homemade beef burgers. Desserts are traditional English treats such as Eton mess and treacle tart. ⓐ 5–7 Castle Road ① 0115 950 1502 ⓦ www.fothergillsnottingham.co.uk ⓛ 11.00–14.00 & 18.00–21.30 Mon–Thur, 11.00–21.30 Fri & Sat, 12.00–16.00 Sun ⓝ Bus: 34, 77, 78

🔵 Give in to temptation at the Walk Café

World Service ££–£££ ㉛ Tucked into a courtyard beside the frontage of historic Newdigate House (where Marshall Tallard, the French commander captured at Blenheim, once lived), World Service exudes laid-back cool. The food is British with a modern flourish, so you might find pan-fried cod with spiced red lentils, or roast chicken served with a garlic risotto. Leave room for puddings like orange posset or chocolate fondant. The lunchtime set menu is good value. ⓐ Newdigate House, Castle Gate ⓣ 0115 847 5587 ⓦ www.worldservicerestaurant.com ⓛ 12.00–14.00 & 19.00–22.00 Mon–Sat, 12.00–14.30 Sun ⓝ Bus: 34, 77, 78

Harts £££ ㉜ Dishes at this acclaimed hotel-restaurant are imaginative modern British and change regularly. Starters might include game terrine, with mains such as roast duck with plums, and carrot cake with pumpkin ice cream for dessert. There is a good value set lunch. ⓐ Standard Hill, Park Row ⓣ 0115 988 1900 ⓦ www.hartsnottingham.co.uk ⓛ Lunch 12.00–13.45 daily; dinner 19.00–21.30 Mon–Thur, 19.00–22.00 Fri & Sat, 19.00–21.00 Sun

Restaurant Sat Bains £££ ㉝ Sat Bains is the gourmet's choice in Nottingham. This acclaimed restaurant with rooms offers five-, seven- and ten-course tasting menus of modern British cuisine. Dishes might include salmon served with cauliflower and nettles, or lamb with lemon and goat's cheese. It's ten minutes in a taxi from the centre of town. ⓐ Lenton Lane ⓣ 0115 986 6566 ⓦ www.restaurantsatbains.com ⓛ 19.00–20.30 daily ⓝ Bus: 13, 14 ⓘ Booking is essential

AFTER DARK

PUBS, BARS & CLUBS

The Canalhouse 34 A converted canal-side warehouse that's now a pub – notable for having part of the canal running through it. Serves pub food and real ales. 🅐 48–52 Canal Street 📞 0115 955 5060

The House of Coco Tang 35 Central chic Nottingham club with a glass block dance floor and rooftop garden. 🅐 45 Bridlesmith Gate 📞 07825 889370 🅦 www.cocotang.co.uk ⓘ Free entry

The Malt Cross 36 This Victorian pub started out as a music hall. It's now a popular venue for live music and functions as a bar/café with a few real ales too. 🅐 16 St James's Street 📞 0115 941 1048 🅦 www.maltcross.com

🔺 *Ye Olde Trip to Jerusalem claims to be England's oldest inn*

NOTTINGHAM'S HISTORIC INNS

Three Nottingham pubs vie for the honour of the label 'oldest pub in England'. Most famous is **Ye Olde Trip to Jerusalem** (ⓐ Brewhouse Yard ⓣ 0115 947 3171), which is cut into the rock beneath Nottingham Castle. The network of caves in which it sits is believed to be medieval, and although the inn was only first mentioned in records in 1618 it's thought there was a medieval brewhouse here. The **Salutation** (ⓐ Hounds Gate, corner with Maid Marian Way ⓣ 0115 988 1948) certainly dates back to the early 15th century, while the **Bell Inn** (ⓐ 18 Angel Row ⓣ 0115 947 5241) sits above a large cave system in a medieval building.

ENTERTAINMENT

Albert Hall ⓪ This striking brick building, built in the style of an Edwardian music hall, hosts recitals, special events and concerts by the likes of Nottingham Symphony Orchestra and Nottingham Philharmonic. ⓐ North Circus Street ⓣ 0115 950 0411 ⓦ www.alberthallnottingham.co.uk

Nottingham Playhouse ㊳ Plays, dance, music and comedy are staged at this lively theatre, visually notable for Anish Kapoor's large *Sky Mirror* sculpture that sits outside – essentially a huge shiny disc that reflects the sky. ⓐ Wellington Circus ⓣ 0115 941 9419 ⓦ www.nottinghamplayhouse.co.uk

▶ *Clumber Bridge in Clumber Park*

OUT OF TOWN
trips

Southwell & Newstead

The countryside around Nottingham may lack the chocolate-box prettiness of the Cotswolds or the scenic splendour of the Lake District, but it's still well worth exploring. On a day trip from the city you could head northeast to the pretty market town of Southwell, birthplace of the Bramley cooking apple, to see its beautiful Georgian buildings and the famous minster. Perhaps return via Papplewick and finally Newstead Abbey, home to the Romantic poet Lord Byron, as famous for his many love affairs as for his poetry.

GETTING THERE

Bus 100 operates a service from Nottingham to Southwell, which takes roughly an hour. Alternatively, go by car, leaving Nottingham on the A612. From Southwell, follow the B6386 to join the A614 (going north) off which you'll be able to reach Papplewick Pumping Station. From here, pick up the A60, to make your way to Newstead Abbey.

SIGHTS & ATTRACTIONS

SOUTHWELL

Southwell Minster This famous attraction was built in the 12th century on the site of a Roman villa, fragments of which can still be seen in the church today. Completed around 1300, the building has a fine Norman nave, while its Chapter House is famed for its glorious stone carvings of foliage – popularly known as the Leaves

Southwell Minster: notable for its 'pepperpot' spires

of Southwell. Look out for the 28 wooden mice on the cathedral's pews and furniture, hand-carved by the famous Yorkshire craftsman Robert 'Mousey' Thompson. **ⓐ** Church Street **ⓣ** 01636 812649 **ⓦ** www.southwellminster.org.uk **ⓛ** Daily

The Workhouse This Victorian workhouse on the outskirts of Southwell is the best preserved in the country and gives a fascinating insight into the lives of the 19th-century poor. Inside, see the dormitories, cellars and work yards – where men and women were segregated. **ⓐ** Upton Road **ⓣ** 01636 817260 **ⓦ** www.nationaltrust.org.uk/workhouse **ⓛ** 12.00–17.00 Wed–Sun (Mar–end Oct), guided tours only **ⓘ** Admission charge

PAPPLEWICK

Papplewick Pumping Station A visit to a water works might seem strange, but this beautifully preserved Victorian pumping station, with the original beam engines built by James Watt and Co, is a stunning example of 19th-century craftsmanship. On certain Sundays you can watch the steam-powered mechanisms in action. **ⓐ** Off Longdale Lane, Ravenshead (off the A60) **ⓣ** 0115 963 2938 **ⓦ** www.papplewickpumpingstation.co.uk **ⓛ** 11.00–14.00 Sun (Apr–Oct) **ⓘ** Admission charge

St James's Church Some think that this church, which dates back to the 12th century, has links with the legend of Robin Hood. Slabs on the floor are carved with bows and arrows and a horn, and they say that the outlaw used yew from the churchyard to make his bows. **ⓐ** Church Lane, off Main Street

NEWSTEAD

Newstead Abbey The abbey started life in the 12th century as an Augustinian priory and flourished until Henry VIII's dissolution of the monasteries. It was given to the wealthy Byron family, who retained many of the building's ecclesiastical features when they turned it into their family seat. When Lord Byron inherited the property in the early 19th century, it was in a state of disrepair and most of its contents had been sold to raise money. He lived in the crumbling mansion with a tamed bear, a wolf and several dogs, and spent his time writing, drinking claret and practising fencing with friends from university. Eventually, when Byron went into exile in Europe, Newstead Abbey was sold. Today you can see the private apartments of this literary bad boy and explore the abbey's glorious grounds. ⓐ Ravenshead, 19 km (12 miles) north of Nottingham on the A60 ⓣ 01623 455900 ⓦ www.nottinghamcity.gov.uk/newsteadabbey ⓛ House: 12.00–17.00 Fri–Mon (Apr–Sept). Grounds: 09.00–16.30 daily ⓝ Pronto buses run from Victoria Bus Station to the abbey gates ⓘ Admission charge

TAKING A BREAK

The Saracen's Head Hotel ££ This picturesque coaching inn dates back to the 16th century and Charles I stayed here during the Civil War. The restaurant serves dishes such as curried fish cakes, beef with tarragon mash, and lamb cutlets with braised celery. ⓐ Market Place, Southwell ⓣ 01636 812701 ⓦ www.saracensheadhotel.net ⓛ Lunch and dinner: daily

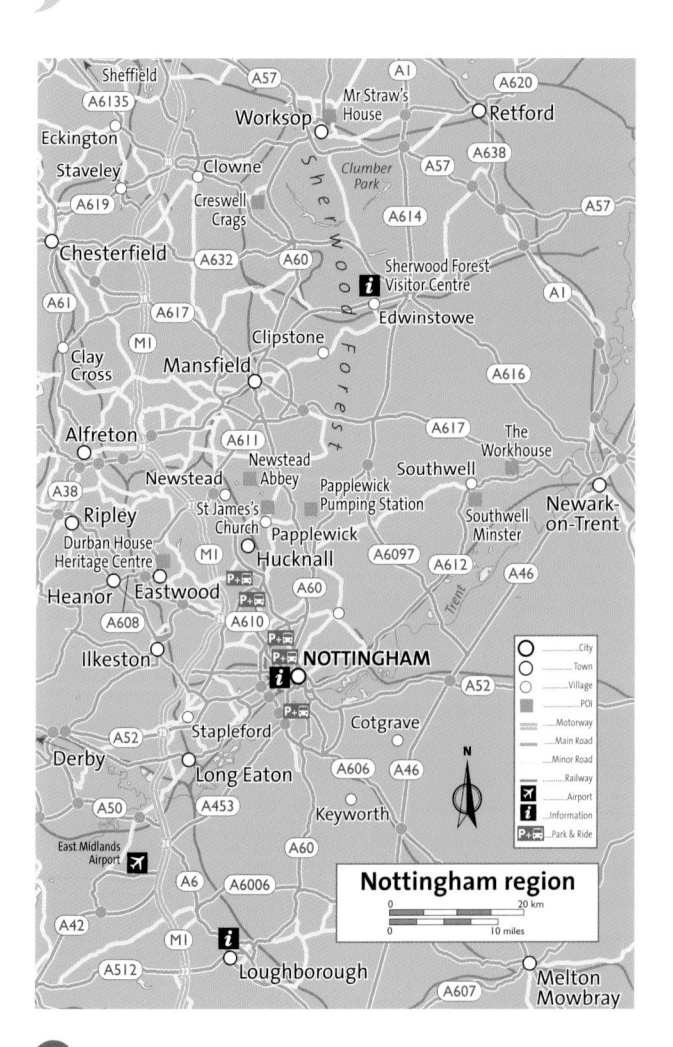

Nottingham region

Sherwood Forest & D H Lawrence country

It's impossible to think of Nottingham without also thinking of Robin Hood and D H Lawrence. On this trip you can take in sights associated with them both – as well as some astonishing prehistoric cave paintings, a glorious landscape garden and a house that's a pre-war time warp.

GETTING THERE

The A614 runs north from Nottingham to Sherwood Forest. After making the acquaintance of the Major Oak you could drive north of the forest to visit Clumber Park, then continue to Worksop to see Mr Straw's House. From Worksop pick up the A60 and drive south, turning onto the B6042 to see Cresswell Crags. Rejoin the A60 and continue south until the turn off for the A611. Eastwood is a few miles from here, off the A608.

SIGHTS & ATTRACTIONS

SHERWOOD FOREST

Sherwood Forest Visitor Centre Sherwood Forest is, of course, steeped in the legend of Robin Hood, the outlaw who stole from the rich to give to the poor. The forest is a great place for a day out, with various activities, including nature trails, walks and cycle routes. Much of the forest is a national nature reserve and it's home to over 900 ancient oak trees. The most famous of these is the 800-year-old Major Oak, which has a hollow centre and a massive girth of 10 m (33 ft). ⓐ Edwinstowe, 27 km (17 miles) north of Nottingham on the A614 ⓣ 01623 823202 ⓦ www.nottinghamshire.gov.uk ⓛ Visitor Centre open 10.00–17.00 (summer); 10.30–16.30 (winter) ⓝ Bus: Sherwood Arrow bus 33 runs from Nottingham to Edwinstowe; the Visitor Centre is a ten-minute walk from there

Clumber Park In the very north of Sherwood Forest is Clumber Park, a 1,537-hectare (3,800-acre) estate that's superb for walks, cycle rides and picnics. The park is a mix of formal, landscaped grounds and woodland, and has a walled kitchen garden with colourful herbaceous borders and a huge glasshouse. There is also a Victorian chapel, a shop and a café. ⓐ 7 km (4 miles) southeast of Worksop ⓣ 01909 544917 ⓦ www.nationaltrust.org.uk ⓛ 10.00–16.00 daily (Nov–Mar);

◬ *The Major Oak: the fabled shelter of Robin Hood and his merry men*

10.00–17.00 (Mar–end Oct) Ⓝ Sherwood Forester bus runs here from Nottingham ❶ Admission charge

Mr Straw's House North of Sherwood Forest is this Edwardian semi where William Straw and his brother were brought up and lived throughout their lives – rarely throwing anything away. The house is still much as they left it: a fascinating time warp with photographs, dark wooden furniture, clothes and china. The interior decorations date back to 1923. ⓐ 7 Blyth Grove, Worksop, off B6045 ❶ 01909 482380 Ⓦ www.nationaltrust.org.uk ⓛ 11.00–17.00 Tues–Sat (mid-Mar–end Oct) ❶ Admission charge. Entry only by timed tickets, which must be pre-booked

Creswell Crags To the west of Sherwood Forest, just on the Derbyshire border, this archaeological site is home to the only known Ice Age cave art in Britain. The images date back 13,000 years and show creatures such as bison, birds and horses. ⓐ Crags Road, Welbeck ❶ 01909 720378 Ⓦ www.creswell-crags.org.uk ⓛ 10.00–17.30 daily (Mar–Sept); 10.00–16.30 daily (Oct and Feb); Sat & Sun only (Nov–Jan). Cave tours only at weekends and in school holidays ❶ Admission charge

D H LAWRENCE COUNTRY
Durban House Heritage Centre, Eastwood Northwest of Nottingham city centre is the former mining town of Eastwood, where D H Lawrence was born and brought up. Take a guided tour of 8a Victoria Street, the house where he was born, and visit Durban House Heritage Centre, which tells the story of his life

and works. ⓐ Durban House, Mansfield Road, Eastwood, off the A610 ⓣ 01773 717353 ⓦ www.broxtowe.gov.uk ⓛ 10.00–16.00 Tues–Fri & Sun (until 17.00 Apr–Oct) ⓘ Admission charge

ACCOMMODATION

Browns £ This award-winning B&B in an 18th-century cottage, has three en-suite guest rooms and a pretty garden. It makes a relaxing base from which to explore the northern parts of Nottinghamshire. ⓐ The Old Orchard Cottage, Holbeck, nr Worksop ⓣ 01909 720659 ⓦ www.brownsholbeck.co.uk

Forest Lodge Hotel £ Very conveniently situated for visiting Sherwood Forest, this family-run 18th-century coaching inn has comfortable rooms and a restaurant. It's in the village of Edwinstowe. ⓐ 2–4 Church Street, Edwinstowe ⓣ 01623 824443 ⓦ www.forestlodgehotel.co.uk

HIRE A CANAL BOAT
For something completely different you could hire a canal boat for a week and cruise the waterways of Nottinghamshire. ⓐ Sawley Marina, Long Eaton ⓣ 0800 3893022 ⓦ www.hireacanalboat.co.uk

ⓘ *If in doubt, try Nottingham Tourism Centre*

PRACTICAL
information

Directory

GETTING THERE

Nottingham is in the heart of England and easy to reach by air, train and road. There are two airports reasonably close to Nottingham, though the one with the most convenient links to the city centre is East Midlands Airport. Robin Hood Airport, just to the north of the county, is closer to Sherwood Forest.

East Midlands Airport (ⓐ Castle Donington, Derby ⓣ 0871 919 9000 ⓦ www.eastmidlandsairport.com) is served by the following airlines:

bmi ⓣ 0844 8484 888 ⓦ www.flybmi.com

bmibaby ⓣ 0905 8282828 ⓦ www.bmibaby.com

Ryanair ⓣ 0871 246 0000 ⓦ www.ryanair.com

Thomsonfly ⓣ 0871 231 4787 ⓦ www.flights.thomson.co.uk

Airlines operating from **Robin Hood Airport** (ⓐ First Avenue, Doncaster ⓣ 0871 220 2210 ⓦ www.robinhoodairport.com) include:

Aer Lingus ⓣ 0871 718 5000 ⓦ www.aerlingus.com

easyJet ⓣ 0905 821 0905 ⓦ www.easyjet.com

Flybe ⓣ 0871 700 2000 ⓦ www.flybe.com

Many people are aware that air travel emits CO_2, which contributes to climate change. You may be interested in the possibility of lessening the environmental impact of your flight through the charity **Climate Care** (ⓦ www.jpmorganclimatecare.com), which offsets your CO_2 by funding environmental projects around the world.

Nottingham is equally well connected to London by rail, as well as to other UK cities. The railway station is just ten minutes' walk from the Old Market Square.

East Midlands Trains ☎ 08457 125678
ⓦ www.eastmidlandstrains.co.uk
National Rail Enquiries ☎ 08457 48 49 50
ⓦ www.nationalrail.co.uk
Traveline ☎ 0871 200 2233 ⓦ www.traveline.org.uk

    Although you wouldn't want to drive inside the city itself, Nottingham is easily reached by car. The M1, A1 and A52 all pass close to the city. For further information, see ⓦ www.nottinghamcity.gov.uk

GETTING AROUND

Easily the best way to get around Nottingham is on foot, as it's a small city and much of its centre is pedestrianised. However there is also a tram, running north–south and passing the Old Market Square, and many buses that cover all parts of the city. The main bus station is Broadmarsh, with another at the Victoria Centre.

NET Tram Travel Centre ☎ 0115 950 6070
ⓦ www.thetram.net ⓔ travelcentre@nctx.co.uk
Nottingham Buses ☎ 0155 950 6070 ⓦ www.nctx.co.uk
Trent Barton Buses ☎ 0177 371 2265 ⓦ www.trentbarton.co.uk
ⓔ enquiries@trentbarton.co.uk
For information about bus routes, contact the **Nottingham Travel Centre** ⓐ 5 South Parade, Old Market Square ☎ 0115 950 6070 🕓 08.00–18.00 Mon, 08.00–17.00 Tues–Fri, 09.00–15.30 Sat. Call Centre open 08.00–19.00 Mon–Sat, 09.00–17.00 Sun

    For more information on getting around Nottingham, including details on bike hire, car hire and taxis, see pages 32–40.

HEALTH, SAFETY & CRIME

Nottingham has, in recent years, acquired a reputation as a city with a high crime rate. However, crime figures have fallen significantly since 2009, and it is worth noting that most crime is concentrated on the outskirts rather than the city centre. Take sensible precautions, as you would in any city.

Hospital/A & E facilities are at **QMC** (Queen's Medical Centre) ⓐ Derby Road ⓣ 0115 924 9924 ⓦ www.nuh.nhs.uk For GP services, contact **NHS Direct** ⓣ 0845 46 47 and for dentists ⓣ 0845 603 1407. **Nottingham NHS Trust** ⓣ 0800 183 0456 ⓦ www.nottinghamcity-pct.nhs.uk

OPENING HOURS

Opening hours are much the same as in other UK cities with shops open 09.00–17.30 Mon–Sat, with late opening on Wednesdays until around 19.00 or 20.00. Most large stores also open on Sundays 10.00–16.00. Some smaller shops close on Monday.

TOILETS

There are public toilets on Greyhound Street as well as in Westfield Broadmarsh and the Victoria Centre. Several large shops and department stores (John Lewis, Debenhams, Marks and Spencer) have their own facilities too.

CHILDREN

Nottingham is pretty family friendly. City-centre attractions that children might enjoy include the City of Caves (see page 67) and (for older children) the Galleries of Justice Museum (see page 48).

Outside the centre there is, of course, Sherwood Forest, in which there is an activity centre, **Adrenalin Jungle** (🕿 01623 883980 🔘 www.adrenalinjungle.com), which offers activities ranging from archery to karting. There is also a **Go Ape High Wire Forest Adventure** (🔘 www.goape.co.uk) in the forest. Westfield Broadmarsh and the Victoria Centre both have baby-changing facilities.

TRAVELLERS WITH DISABILITIES

Nottingham City Council's website has information on access to specific attractions at 🔘 www.nottinghamcity.gov.uk. Access varies with the nature of the building, as in other parts of the UK. There is an access team number 🕿 0115 915 3692. There is a special Changing Places toilet on Greyhound Street, off Old Market Square.

FURTHER INFORMATION

Nottingham Tourism Centre 🅰 1–4 Smith Row, nr Old Market Square 🕿 08444 77 5678 🔘 www.visitnotts.com
🅔 tourist.information@nottinghamcity.gov.uk
Sherwood Forest Visitor Centre 🅰 Sherwood Forest Country Park, Edwinstowe 🕿 01623 823202
🔘 www.nottinghamshire.gov.uk/sherwoodforest
🅔 sherwood.forest@nottscc.gov.uk

ACKNOWLEDGEMENTS

The photographs in this book were taken by Zenna West for Thomas Cook Publishing, to whom the copyright belongs, except for the following: City of Caves, Nottingham page 68; Experience Nottingham pages 26–7, 29, 79, 81 & 86; JMS Photography page 21.

Project and copy editor: Kate Taylor
Proofreaders: Rachel Norridge & Michele Greenbank
Layout: Trevor Double
Indexer: Marie Lorimer

AUTHOR BIOGRAPHY

Rebecca Ford is an award-winning travel journalist who writes for national newspapers and magazines, covering everything from railway journeys to wildlife tours. She has written several guidebooks and contributed to many more – including titles on Italy and eco-travel. She also writes scripts for audio-guides.

Send your thoughts to
books@thomascook.com

- Found a great bar, club, shop or must-see sight that we don't feature?
- Like to tip us off about any information that needs a little updating?
- Want to tell us what you love about this handy little guidebook and more importantly how we can make it even handier?

Then here's your chance to tell all! Send us ideas, discoveries and recommendations today and then look out for your valuable input in the next edition of this title.

Email the above address (stating the title) or write to:
pocket guides Series Editor, Thomas Cook Publishing, PO Box 227, Coningsby Road, Peterborough PE3 8SB, UK.